Seven Crazy Days on Maui

Seven Crazy Days on Maui

A True Story of Wonder & Woe

Paul Samuel Dolman

South Beach

SOUTH BEACH PUBLISHING

Published by South Beach (USA)

404 Sweet Magnolia Court

Saint Augustine, Florida 32080

First printing, June 2016

Copyright © 2016 by Paul Samuel Dolman

All rights reserved. No part of this book may be reproduced, scanned, or distributed in any printed or electronic form without permission. Please do not participate in or encourage piracy of copyrighted materials in violation of the author's rights. Purchase only authorized editions.

LIBRARY OF CONGRESS CATALOGING-IN-PUBLICATION DATA

ISBN 978-1-890115-03-6

Printed in the United States of America
Cover Designed by Matthew Wayne Selznick

While the author has made every effort to provide accurate telephone numbers, Internet addresses, and other contact information at the time of publication, neither the publisher nor the author assumes any responsibility for errors or for changes that occur after publication. Further, the publisher does not have any control over and does not assume any responsibility for author or third-party websites or their content

For All The Amazing Women

In my Life

My Life giving Mother

My Healer Bonnie Johnson

My Spirit Guide Katherine Lott

My Sweet Sisters-

Annie, Brenda, Karen, Scarlet

I STILL BELIEVE IN MIRACLES

Seven Crazy Days On Maui

By Paul Samuel Dolman

A true story of wonder & woe

As the plane makes its makes its final approach into paradise the window seat view takes away my breath.

Out here in the midst of all this endless water sits a tiny green jewel. The lime green sea glistens along golden sand beaches, as two mountains reach majestically towards the sky above.

As my sandal-clad feet touch the ground, I feel a strange sense of having been here before.

The air on my skin feels warm and alive. I take a few deep breaths and let the fragrant sea breezes fill me.

An old faded blue taxi van approaches along the airport curb and the dark-skinned driver asks, "Hey Boss, you need a ride?"

I nod, "Yes." I throw my small bag in ahead of me and climb aboard. "So where should I go?"

He lowers his sunglasses, looks back, raises an eyebrow and says, "You have no destination?"

"Well, I figured the hard part was simply getting here. It's my first time and I don't have a plan." I look up at a brilliant sun. "Are you a native of the island?"

"I am. Seventh generation. How long are you planning to be here?"

"I bought a one-way ticket, so I have no idea."

His head moves slightly, "You're not a crazy person are you?"

"Yes, unfortunately I am, but not in a normal crazy way."

He looks at me suspiciously in his mirror. "So *not normal crazy?*"

"Yes."

He takes a moment to process the unfolding events. "Not to be too personal, but do you have any money?"

"Oh yes, more than enough." I pat my pocket. "Would you like to see my stash?"

He pauses and looks at me intensely. "No, I trust you."

I then sweep my hand across a stunning vista. "Last night I was in the heart of Los Angeles and found myself with a wide open schedule. Something silent within me said, 'How about Maui?' I bought a ticket online and then spent the whole night daydreaming."

"Daydreaming at night. I like that." There is the trace of a smile. "Maui, she draws people here."

I take an exceptionally long breath. "The air is so clear."

"It's the trade winds, they blow strongly and often."

"Look, I know I'll end up in a hotel soon enough, but maybe you know somewhere special to start my adventure?"

"Special?"

"You know, a hallowed spot. Is there a mall close by?"

He finally smiles. "Give me a minute to feel your Spirit."

His skin is brown and beautiful, his hair long dark with streaks of silver, his hands calloused, his manner thoughtful and deliberate. There is an air of kindness about him. My guess is he is somewhere in his fifties. He closes his eyes quite seriously and then puts the taxi in gear. "All set."

"Wait, I never got your name."

"Pomaika'i. But call me Kai."

"Doesn't Kai mean blessing?"

"Yes. Pomaika'i is blessing in Hawaiian."

We shake hands firmly. "Paul."

Kai breaks into a broad grin. "Ok then Boss, let's find you some aloha."

We drive slowly along a postcard-worthy landscape of drop dead gorgeous views and lava-shrouded lagoons.

"Brother Kai, I'm sorry if I threw you back there, but in my world things tend to work out better when I just stay open and let the magic happen."

"No worries, my friend. No worries."

His finger is directed at what looks like one of the mountains shrouded in a mysterious cloak of blue-gray clouds. "That's Haleakala."

"A mountain?"

He shakes his head. "A volcano. The ancients said that was the home to the grandmother of the God Maui… that she helped him capture the sun to slow its journey across the sky… so the days could be longer and brighter. Haleakala means 'House of the Sun.' It's about 10,000 feet high and her mass covers about 75% of Maui. If you go up there, dress warmly. Even in the heart of summer, it can be really cold at the peak."

I look off towards the top then down a long, lush valley. "Maui looks a lot bigger than I had imagined."

He looks back at me in his mirror. "It's about 730 square miles, give or take."

"Can a guy hitchhike?"

"In some places, but it can be hard as a haole."

I lean forward. "A what?"

"A haole…"

"Howl-ee? What's that?"

He turns towards me. "A white person."

"What a great nickname. What does it mean when translated? Piece of shit?"

Kai laughs loudly. "Brother, that is the funniest thing I have heard in a long, long time. Actually it means 'without breath.' The white settlers who stole these islands from my people were without breath."

"One could almost say… without spirit."

"You could declare that. Spirit is breath, yes."

I shake my head and look across rich green fields. "Manifest Destiny means I can come and steal everything because the god I made up conveniently says I am entitled to take it."

He reaches back a hand to slap me five. "I like that too." He raises his arm towards the green sea. "The original people came here thousands of years ago from the South Seas of Polynesia in wooden canoes."

"In canoes? How in heaven's name did they find it?"

"They followed the stars and migrating birds north, thinking there must be land in that direction. They were very brave."-

We pull down a street filled with small shops that runs along the water. "This is Front Street in Lahaina. This used to be the capital of Hawaii before Honolulu. It is where all the whaling ships used to launch."

I look towards the sea. "Are there whales here?"

"Lots and lots of humpbacks. They come all the way from Alaska to have their babies. If you keep your eyes on the ocean, you will see them." We pull over. "Check out this tree." He gestures towards the largest banyan tree I have ever seen.

"Good lord, this colossus almost takes up the whole block."

Kai sticks his head out the window and looks up into her myriad of tangled branches. "That is supposed to be the oldest tree in all of Hawaii. Some missionaries planted her back in the late 1800s. I feel like this is where you are supposed to start your trip."

"Oh, good thinking...thank you. It looks like the Home Tree in the movie *Avatar*. Can I get out and touch it?"

"Absolutely. That's why I brought you here. Go ask Maui to give you an aloha welcome."

I hesitate for a moment.

He points towards the banyan. "Go ahead, Boss. Don't worry, the meter is not running. You're Kama'aina now."

"Kam…"

"Kama'aina. You are a local, which means you get the local discount. But it must be offered, never asked for."

"Thank you." I shake his hand.

"No worries, Boss. Now go talk to the tree."

Wandering over, I'm struck by the scope of this gigantic being. My hand reaches out and gently touches the Mahatma. *'Okay Maui, I am in your hands now. Please be gentle, loving, and allow me to taste your pleasures. Teach me a thing or two, keep me safe, and let me love. Thank you for welcoming me to your shores. Thank you.'*

There are a few moments of silence and then I wander back to the cab.

After a few moments without words, my guide says, "Well done, Boss."

"I have to say I think I felt a wave of something."

"Really?"

"But it might just be a little gas from all the flying."

He chuckles and shakes his head. "Oh, Boss, you will do well here. Come on, I'll take you over to Paia. There is a sweet little motel there that is affordable, convenient and clean."

We drive awhile in silence, which seems appropriate in the presence of such natural beauty. My guide points toward the colorful imagery and says quietly, "There are between 23 and 29 microclimates in Maui, depending on who one talks to. I tend to believe it's at least 29!"

He points towards green fields that stretch for miles. "Sugar cane. The sugar companies own most of the land here. It's sad. The cane is brutal for the soil and when they burn, it's bad for the eyes."

The sun breaks through a series of mountains and shines a river of light upon the hillside.

In the distance a rainbow appears.

"My God, this island is so surreal." I whisper.

"That is the Elan Valley. It is considered very holy ground. Back in the 1800s, Queen Kaʻahumanu would go to the high ground to look out across her kingdom. She was a great leader and they were a proud people."

A few minutes later we pass a shopping area called, 'The Queen Kaʻahumanu Center.' "Wait, did the haoles steal all this land then name a strip mall after the Queen?"

He frowns and shakes his head. "Yes, they did."

"The absurdity of the white man never ceases to amaze me."

He shifts the conversation. "Boss, may I ask what your passion is?"

"As in what do I do?"

He nods. "Call it what you will."

"I guess I am a writer now. My book, *Hitchhiking With Larry David* was just bought and will be released in hardcover in June."

"A writer who got published in my cab? Many blessings, brother. That is fantastic, but who is Larry David?"

I shake my head. "Just a guy on television…"

"Forgive me. I never watch that little box of horrors. It feels bad for my spirit."

"The book is also a love story."

He looks back at me in his rearview mirror. "Yours?"

I nod.

He smiles. "There's always a girl."

I echo him. "Yes sir, there is always a dame."

He looks again in the mirror, "Not to pry and since you are solo, may I ask if you are still together?"

I shake my head no. "Sadly, we are not. It's been a couple years since we split, but man, she's been a tough one to get over. That women left a piece of herself in here." I point towards my chest. "If it's not gone by the time I leave here, I'm going to Salem for an exorcism."

He nods. "I'm sorry about that boss. Love takes time; loss takes longer."

I reach out and pat his shoulder. "Brother you are a shaman. Your words are very wise."

Love takes time; loss takes longer.

He modestly deflects my praise. "Hand-me-down wisdom, my friend. Old-school stuff. The waters of Maui should be healing for you as will the abundance of beautiful ladies moving about." He gestures towards two lovely bikini-clad gals chatting on the sidewalk. "There are many goddesses here."

I nod. "The pull of life's beauty never gets old."

We end up in a funky little surf town with a bunch of worn down buildings. As we pull in front of an old two-story flophouse, he says, "Home sweet home, Boss." He grabs my bag and makes a funny face. "Is there anything in here?"

"Just a few tee shirts, a pair of old shorts... I like to travel light."

"I'll say." He picks it up and down again.

I peel off some serious cash and hand it to him.

"I appreciate the tour and I am off to a good start, thanks to you."

He takes a look at the money. "No, this is way too much. I can't take all this."

"Yes, you can. Besides, it's all stolen anyway. You might as well spend it before they catch up to me."

He smiles but is still hesitant.

"Do you have kids?"

"Grandkids. I am seventy-six years young."

This shocks me. "What? Really? Have you had any work done? A facelift?" I say while refusing the money he is trying to hand me. "You look amazing."

"I live a clean life and my spirit is light of worry."

"Yes, but with all that family, you're probably broke, so spend it on them. I have more than enough. Can we hug it out?"

"Of course. Come here. Heart to heart."

I pick up my bag. "OK Kai, you better get out of here while you can. If word gets out you were hugging a haole, there will be hell to pay."

He smiles. "Mahalo, my friend."

"Means…"

"Thank you."

"Mahalo Brother Kai."

He holds up the money. "Can I buy your book online?"

I smile. "Yes, you can."

He waves to me as his old rig pulls away.

After a great night's sleep, I go for a little morning exploration. Paia is a two-street town with a couple of cafes, three or four restaurants, and a few tee shirt shops. An old man directs me to Anthony's for some serious locally grown espresso that gets my brain's attention.

The town is loaded with hippies and people who look semi-homeless. I see guys older than me whose primary mode of transportation is riding a skateboard. Surfers are plentiful since the waves along the north shore are legendary. One guy with more tattoos than I can count talks about seeing the iconic wave rider Laird Hamilton out on the water the previous morning.

An hour later I decide to grab a little grub at a small place just off the main drag. After placing my order, a very tall distinguished gentleman, who looks vaguely familiar, sits down alone at the table next to me. A few people greet him politely as if he is royalty. He catches me taking this in and nods.

"You must be the mob boss," I quip.

He grins and extends his hand. "Do you live here?"

"Not yet. I arrived yesterday. This is my first time here and I am already in love with the place."

"Well then, aloha. How long do you plan to stay?"

"At least a couple of months. Are you a resident?"

"Yes, part of the time. I own a restaurant in Lahaina. You should come by sometime; it's called Fleetwoods." He reaches out to shake my hand again. "I'm Mick."

Oh yeah!

"My name is Paul." I sweep my hand across the sky and ask, "How do you like it here?"

"I love it. There is nothing quite like Maui."

After a couple of minutes he finishes his java. "Well, I have to run along. It was so nice to meet you. I hope the island welcomes you warmly."

"Mahalo, Mick. Oh and by the way, you guys made some beautiful music."

He smiles. "How kind of you." He shakes my hand. "Have a lovely day."

After a long walk and another swim, my hunger leads me into a bustling local grocery store.

Mana Health Foods is an oasis of excellent food, organic supplies, and the most beautiful hippie girls I have ever seen. I grab some steamed veggies and watch an endless parade of healthy, glowing gals come and go.

After a month in Hollywood, these Earth Queens with their easy smiles and sandy, bare feet are a welcome antidote to the jaded babes of Beverly Hills cloaked in pretention, botox, and designer label attitudes.

My daydreams take me far and near until a guy wanders up and asks me to sign some kind of petition (Will I support a living wage for skateboarding?). In the distance another rainbow appears above the ocean.

Boy, I could get used to this.

The locals are abuzz about a huge swell bringing gigantic waves of over sixty feet to a beach up the road.

I decide to check it out and stick out my thumb. Within a minute I am sitting in the back of an old pickup truck with a couple of surfers as we wind our way along the north shore to a mythical stretch of beach called Jaws.

The sky is radiant blue and my view is lush. We pass a bamboo forest, some strange trees with colorful stripes, and stunning vistas of the sea.

Turning off the road, we park the old heap and then walk down towards the ocean. Though far away, I can already hear the roar of the surf. My heart races and my pace quickens, drawn by the primal energy emanating from Mother Ocean.

What will sixty-foot waves look like up close?

When we reach the coast I am in shock to see small human forms paddling along on boards, out amongst the deep blue giants.

Here on a bluff, a fairly large crowd has gathered to take it all in. Even at a safe distance, the size and power of the surf is humbling.

The swell is epic and it sends in its white-capped troops towards the shore in endless sets. The wind howls into my face as I watch these mythic water creatures crest and then crash upon the coast.

I see in them the metaphor of birth and death for our own brief existence.

After a couple hours of awe, it's time to head home.

On the way back, I end up hitching a ride in a very old VW Van. My classic hippie-driver guide gives me the Maui lowdown, "Bro, the north shore is way too wet and wild. You want to be in Kihei."

"How come?"

"It never rains, the beaches are golden, there is tons of great weed, and a whole lot of hot girls walking around in bikinis. I'm headed there now. Come catch a sunset with The Dude."

I think about it for a nano-second or two then say, "What the hell. Why not?"

Hippie Man slaps me a high-five. "Road trip!"

With a wide assortment of noises and grinding, our dilapidated shaggin' wagon labors mightily to make the twenty-mile trek across the island.

After some strange hissing, I point in the direction of the engine and ask, "Do you think we'll actually make it?"

"Man, let's hope so. She never lets me down. But this poor old beast might be on her last legs."

"Sometimes lately I feel the same way about my own form. I think God dropped the cosmic ball with this whole aging thing. Why can't I remain healthy and vibrant right up to the moment I keel over?"

"Sounds good to my ears." My driver then offers to share some of Maui's finest home grown. "Care for a few hits?"

"No, thanks. I don't smoke. But I love the smell of it."

He looks puzzled. "Wait, you really don't smoke?"

"I was never into any kind of tobacco."

He nods like he is deeply considering this. "Can't remember meeting anyone who didn't smoke here. Wait... oh no, she did." There is a long pause. "Oh well, more for the rest of us." With that The Dude takes another hit on the doobie.

The Dude and I park the rusty bus on a semi-deserted beach and take in a truly vibrant display of ethereal light and color.

I point down the shore. "Brother, you were right. This side is much calmer. I dig it."

He takes out a card and writes a number on the back. "Call my friend Jack. He has a little ohana for rent right down the street and it is only about a block off the beach."

"Ohana? What's that, a tent?"

He takes a long hit of weed then waves me off. "No Bro, it's a little guest house. I forgot you are a newbie here. You'll get the lingo down soon." He then lets out a long, slow exhale. "Man, this is some seriously good shit."

We watch a whale soar out of the water in the distance and I gasp. "Wow that is an amazing site."

"Agreed. And it never gets old." He takes another long hit then, "Holy, holy! I gotta go pick up my old lady. I totally spaced, and now she is gonna kick my ass sideways. Shit."

"Hey Dude, how do I get back?"

"Hitchhike man. Or just sleep on the beach; it's cool here and the cops don't mind. Peace."

Feeling a bit lost and turned around, I end up calling his friend Jack who supposedly lives somewhere in the vicinity.

A few minutes later a tiny brown skinned man generously rescues me and brings me over to his home.

Once there he shows me a small studio behind the house that is wide open. "Can I move in tomorrow?"

"It is yours." He pats me on the back and refuses a deposit.

With only a single, light bag, my migration the following morning across the rock is a simple one.

Now it's time to get some wheels. Fate complies when I bump into a guy with a red huffy beach cruiser who has to unload this baby by nightfall. The bike is great for local trips but I soon discover I need something with a little more range that can handle the hills.

I opt for a beautiful blue scooter that gets a 100mpg and makes exploring 1000 times more fun.

One cannot begin to communicate the joys of scooter life. No traffic, no parking challenges, cruising up steep hills with ease, $5 a week in gas, ~~the wind in my hair~~, the freedom, the stars, the... ok, ok, I REALLY love my scooter.

With my beloved motor cruiser and everything I ever need within a scant few miles, I am free to enjoy 'Village Life.'

In a village you meet people. You bond with the locals. You get to know the merchants. You are in touch with the street. And, of course, every village has an idiot...

This idyllic morning my scooter purrs along the south shore past ancient fields of dark lava. A local fisherman told me that Haleakala` has only erupted three times in the last nine-hundred years, so there was no need to lose any sleep over a lava disruption.

The water to my right is green and calm. This area, called 'The Dumps', is a famous place to snorkel and well worth the extra drive.

I ease into the water and let my body adjust to the temperature. Maui's surf is relatively warm, but there is always that first gasp of acclimation.

Once under the line between air and ocean, I enter a new world, one of vast colorful creatures and elaborate coral configurations.

Every moment spent in this parallel universe is one of expanded awe. The sheer variety of creatures and colors is mind-blowing.

A small group of art deco adorned fish decides to use me as a sort of floating shield/shelter, rather than sit exposed in the shallow open water. There have been reports of tiger sharks in this area so my primal brain periodically scans the aquatic horizon for any creature larger than myself.

Though as afraid as the next person of these perfect predators, I cannot allow the fear of what is improbable to keep me from the sea of bliss.

This realization is a wonderful metaphor for all of life, finding the balance between practical caution and engaged participation. Physical caution can keep us safe, but spiritual fear will stagnate our growth.

Hovering near a cluster of rocks I catch sight of my first octopus peaking out from a crevice. It is one thing to see this on a television or in an aquarium, but in the wild, wow! These eight-limbed miracles have an advanced brain capacity so incredible that some scientists have half-jokingly referred to them as aliens.

A few minutes later there is a very large, ancient, oval form gliding effortlessly in front of me. In my world, encountering a giant sea turtle is the equivalent to seeing an angel or burning bush. I slowly shadow her with the least amount of intrusion as possible.

Soon there are two more of her kind, though not quite as large, joining us on our jaunt. A fairly large fish swims close to me bathed in pitch black with neon blue markings trailed by two popsicle-yellow angelfish.

I begin to feel like a guest at the Mad Hatter's Undersea Ball.

With the sun's rays careening through the water, I pause to take it all in.

As I look across my floating form, weightless in paradise, my treasured Buddha beads, given to me years ago by a Tibetan Monk, are releasing from my left wrist.

Silently I think, 'Oh no, these must not be lost!'

As I begin to follow their slow motion descent downward I hear the spirit guide within me suggest to let them go.

"Let this be your gift to Mother Maui."

Instinctively, I gather several of the beads in my hand, but the quiet voice gently urges me again.

"Let go. Let go of everything. Always let go."

For a moment I am still and watch the remainder of the small, round wooden totems begin to disappear into the rocks and sand. I slowly extend my hand in a sweeping underwater gesture and release the few beads I have retrieved.

As they all float towards the floor, I say a blessing. 'This is for you, Maui. Thank you for your Aloha and Love. Mahalo, Maui. Mahalo.'

Soon I begin to merge with the deeper Presence within me... knowing all is well and in divine order. How perfect it all is.

There is a silence under the water that is profoundly healing.

I look up to see the largest of the three turtles checking me out and I smile within myself.

Sadly, my time here is done. I must return to the land, the place of my origin and the unconscious noise of my own species. Though reluctant to leave, I turn and head back towards shore, feeling a little lighter than when I entered this submerged kingdom.

~~~

After a couple of weeks in the little bungalow, I move over to a larger house recently rented by an old woman who appears at first to be quite normal.

Ancient Hawaiian Proverb: Don't judge an elderly book by its cover.

About a week after I move in, strange boxes of junk begin to appear randomly around the house.

"What's all this stuff doing here?" I ask.

"I have been keeping all of my things in another place, plus two garages, but the guy there said I had to have it all out by the end of the month. What an asshole."

I look into one of her boxes and see four different old toasters. "How long have you had this stuff over there?"

"Twelve years."

Cue the rim shot!

She is seething and pacing. "He told me months ago I had to get rid of it, but I have nowhere to put it, so I'm stuck. He even called the cops on me twice. It's a mess."

I take a moment to look at more of the contents in the dusty boxes: three broken printers long out of date, a rotary phone, empty jars, vitamins with World War Two era expiration dates, newspapers, magazines, a few snorkels, the odd pot or pan, broken light bulbs... "Only twelve years?"

"Yeah, give or take... hey, be careful with that! It came from India."

I gently place a small plastic Buddha that looks a lot like a cheap cereal prize back in the box. "But what are you going to do with all of this? We can't have it filling up our living quarters. It's already blocking some of the windows and part of the kitchen."

"I'll sort it out. Just give me some time," the Cosmic Hoarder begs, and then looks off into another dimension with a gaze that reminds me of Dustin Hoffman in *Rain Man.*

After another week of expanding clutter, the home's tenants (us) grow united in their hatred for her ways. Not any real hardcore hatred, more of the garden-variety style disdain.

Also, we must avoid being cornered by her at all costs. If caught, you will be subjected to a long rambling monologue about mysteriously missing towels or teaspoons that have somehow vanished on their own accord, her prevailing conspiracy theory being they were stolen by a myriad of enemies, both real and imagined, who are always trying to take advantage of her.

Luckily, The Cosmic Hoarder is more annoying than dangerous and fortunately for the rest of us, tends to vanish for long stretches. During one of her extended absences, I organize my housemates in a spontaneous box moving blitzkrieg. The mass of clutter is moved to the garage for her to deal with sometime over the next twelve years.

The Call

As the brilliant Maui sunshine cascades down upon me unimpeded by a single cloud, I sit on the golden sand and watch a pair of mighty humpback whales breech off the south coast.

My phone vibrates with a number I don't recognize.

"Hello? Hello?"

"Pauly?"

"Yes..."

"I.. I want... I wondered..." I hear the sound of crying and then... "I cannot go on another day like this. I simply do not want to live anymore. I don't... I do not have the energy to keep faking it while surrounded by people who so deeply hate me."

The voice on the other end of the line is raw. The sobs become heavy and heartfelt. The despair is palatable and her breathing shallow, as she tries in vain to regain her frail composure.

"Is that you?" I whisper.

Silence. "Please, give me... I need a moment... to..."

"Sure." The waves in the water come in sets that appear to be in sync with her sobs.

"Pauly, you are the only one who has ever really loved me, seen me, and supported me. I have to find a way back to you. I need to see you again, if only to bask in your bright light."

Long pause…

She continues. "I need to come home. Please let me come home."

The Broken Girl softly weeps as I listen silently. Her primal cries pierce the marble walls I have so meticulously constructed to protect me. Time, distance, neglect, disrespect, insensitivity and deceit have changed none of the powerful feelings connected to this one woman.

My mind drifts back over our barren landscape of wasted years in self-imposed mutual exile. Like a butterfly randomly dancing between flowers, my memory pauses briefly on moments from our past: warm embraces, tender smiles, pettiness, afflictions, addictions and tears.

Flashback:

Through the generosity of friends, I end up housesitting a huge historic home in the heart of Del Mar. The house, built in the 1920s, offers a panoramic view of the Pacific Ocean.

The Del is a quiet little coastal town about thirty miles north of downtown San Diego. It consists of a funky little village of shops and restaurants. The beach is spacious and soft, allowing unimpeded walks beside colorful cliffs.

On my second night, I attend a small dinner party and sit next to an olive-skinned woman whose eyes remind me of the sparkling turquoise waters of the southern Caribbean. In one timeless moment we silently connect and my breathing becomes noticeably shallow.

This is interesting...

After a magical couple of hours filled with rich food, stimulating conversations and collective good cheer, I walk this young woman to her car. The night air is cool and crisp and you can hear the gentle break of the waves down the hill. Under an infinite sea of stars she softly asks, "How long are you staying in Del Mar?"

I look up the radiant celestial dome and inhale the evening. "My guess is about three weeks."

As the sea air blows over us, she pauses as if trying to find the right words. "Not to be too forward or anything, but I feel like I have known you my whole life."

"I know what you mean. Ours feels like one of those rare instances when you meet a stranger and pick up right where you left off."

She leans into me. "Exactly."

~~~

Silently I wonder about my Broken Girl...

Has she finally hit the bottom? Finally? For a moment I wonder about the two of us reuniting, but it feels too late. The part of me that loved her so completely has died a long time ago, not all at once, but from a thousand different cuts.

I am pulled back from my daydream to the present by her gentle whisper, "Are you there?"

"Yes, I'm sorry."

"Pauly, can I please come home?"

Shades

The next morning I sit down on an old wooden bench in front of my favorite Kihei coffee shop. I often grab some espresso here, then walk across the street to the surf's edge and watch the whales frolic in the sunrise sun.

An older man of very slight build, with dirt on deeply sun tanned arms approaches. "What a morning!"

"Another day in paradise."

He is carrying a tattered bag that, just like him, has seen better days. He gracefully gestures at the empty seat beside me, as if to ask permission to occupy the space.

I nod. "Of course…"

This fellow looks like someone who has spent a lot of time in the great outdoors, perhaps more out of necessity than choice. Since we are across the street from the park where many without shelter sleep, I would venture to say he is homeless. While glancing out at the water he asks, "Can I buy you a cup of coffee?"

His simple request surprises me.

"I have no choice but to say yes."

"How come?"

I turn and point towards his head. "You're wearing a Red Sox cap, so I know you've had a lifetime of suffering. It's the least I can do."

He smiles. "Is Boston your team?"

"Yes, sadly. But hey, spring training is around the corner. So hope springs eternal. Maybe this is finally our year."

"It is certainly our day. What a beauty!" He slowly reaches a somewhat shaky hand my way. "Hi, they call me Shades."

I embrace his friendly offering in my palm. "Nice to meet you. They call me a lot of things, some of which I won't repeat, but my name is Paul."

He grins and points towards my cup. "More coffee?"

"Can I buy?"

"Nope. I invited you. You can get the next one."

"Deal."

He vanishes into the store for a few moments and returns with two large containers of brew. "I put some cream in it for you. You look like a cream and a dab of sugar man to me."

"Good call, kind sir. Thank you."

He hands me my cup. "Paul, are you new in these parts?"

"I am but plan to stick around for a couple of months, then it's off to Babylon."

He smiles, "Which is…"

"Los Angeles. How about you?"

He raises his hand, extends a finger towards the park across the street. "Home sweet home."

"It looks like you have a million-dollar view."

He smiles. "Have you been out to Big Beach yet?"

"No…"

Old Shades shakes his head slowly. "There is some powerful juju out there worth soaking in."

"I'll pop out later and check it out."

For a long time we just sit in comfortable silence soaking in the morning and watching the world go by.

Old Shades breaks the silence with a simple question. "Well, young man, is there a woman in your life?"

Flashback:

As the sun wears away a reluctant marine layer, The Broken Girl and I stroll south for miles as giant Torrey Pines on the bluff above us sway slowly in the sea breeze.

"Please tell me about you," I implore. "Give me the scoop."

She shakes her head. "I don't know. Are you sure? I don't want to scare you off."

"Don't worry. I'm only afraid of heights."

She smiles, touches my arm, and let's out a long, slow exhale. "Here is the Reader's Digest version: I am in a bitter fight with my soon-to-be attorney ex-husband. On top of that, I'm flat broke and living with a crazy girlfriend, who might be in love with me, even though she has a boyfriend. I also feel completely lost in my life, and struggle with depression."

There is a moment or two of silence as I allow this to sink in. "Okay, now tell me the bad stuff."

She tilts her head a bit before bursting into laughter. "Thank you. I needed that."

She turns and looks towards the sparkling water as a couple of pelicans silently pass over us. "I was all of twenty-two when I got married and then we separated a couple of times and got back together."

I put my hand on her shoulder. "And now..."

She makes a strange face then looks away from me. "If I tell you the truth, you might turn around and walk in the other direction."

I put my hand on her shoulder. "That would be one lonely walk by myself."

She manages a faint smile.

I touch her arm. "Try me."

"There is a rich older man who wants to buy me a home in Beverly Hills, a white Range Rover, and take care of me as his mistress."

"How old are we talking?"

"Maybe late 60s or even 70. It's hard for me to share that with you."

"How old are you?"

"I just turned 26. He's been very generous to me. In two weeks I am supposed to go with him to Europe and stay on his yacht. Last month, he put me up at the Beverly Hills hotel for a week and bought me all kinds of presents."

She pauses for a moment and bends down to pick up a shell. A beautiful Golden Retriever barks 'good morning' from the back deck of an enormous home.

She looks at the sea and then at me. "Do you want to walk away?"

The question catches me off guard. "Why?"

"For being with him."

"God no, but the idea of you with him makes me sad because you are so amazing. I think you deserve to be loved, not leased."

We then walk a long while holding hands and without words. The surf gently caresses the shore, with the light dancing off each utterly unique sequence of waves.

In the midst of my time with her, I have a sudden realization: my for-as-long-I-can-remember- hopelessly empty... forever-lonely-even-in-a-crowd... Siamese-Twin Self has gone missing. "Heavens, where is The Hole?"

Does The Hole's absence have anything to do with this Green Eyed Goddess walking silently beside me?

Perhaps...

~~~

I break our wordless reverie. "Shades, do you mind if I ask you for a little advice."

He says nothing before slowly unfurling his hand.

"I once was deeply in love with a woman who touched in me a place I did not know existed. The love was both powerful and destructive, the highs were as epic as the lows were crippling. In the end, I realized I loved a person who did not love herself, and that our struggle for union would never become a cohesive force for our mutual good.

A few years ago we parted. Yesterday, she resurfaced with her life in shambles and asked, through suffering and sobs, if she could come back to me, to join me here in Maui."

He raises his hand to stop me. "First, you need to be honest with yourself and admit that you still love her."

"How do you know that I do?"

"I can hear it in your voice. The plaintive ache, the longing, the regret, the what-might-have-been… it is all there, especially in the space between the words."

A bit stunned, I sit for a moment in silence and consider his pronouncement. A deep exhale, a small sigh, and then, "Yes, I guess I do. I've been trying to deny this to myself. I do not want to love this woman."

He takes a slow sip of coffee then says almost in a whisper. "You don't have a choice, brother. We don't choose who we love any more than we can decide what the weather is going to be today. Your mind might say 'hell no,' but your heart finds something in her that is beautiful and that transcends all of her crazy-ass bullshit. Once our hearts truly dance with someone, that particular song belongs to them and them alone."

I feel a warm tear run down my right cheek.

He pats my leg. "There you go. It's important to feel everything fully and not play it too safe. Raw emotion is a sign of a healthy life."

I wipe away the water on my face and try to recover a little. "Thank you."

He looks off to the sea and then down at the ground. "Do you have any desire to rekindle a relationship with her?"

"Not in the current state of who she is, no. I realize the person I loved for a time, the girl I met in Del Mar and lived with in Nashville, is long gone."

"And if you brought her here…"

"I don't know how I could pull that off without completely destroying my own peace."

He reflects for a few moments while gazing out across the endless waters of the mighty Pacific. "Then let it stew for a few. Don't rush in or run away. One thing is for sure, whatever unfolds is going to grow and teach you. One of my life mantras is 'lean towards love,' but never at the expense of your values."

I let that sink in. "Lean towards love. I like that."

He stands up. "Well, young man, I have enjoyed this very much. Time and tide wait for no man. We will do it again. I am here most mornings, unless I'm not…"

I rise too. "We shall, and next time, it's my turn to buy."

"I'm going to hold you to that." He starts to walk away, gets about ten yards, pauses, and then turns around. "Oh, one more thing."

"Yes?"

"Life's short, so stay out of the shade." He dons his cap, does a slight bow, and moves on.

The Sage and the Star

Feeling inspired I head over to the north shore and then up the mountain on Baldwin Avenue to the Lumeria Retreat Center. I have heard there is a daily meditation here led by a Sage named Claudio.

The sanctuary is perched on a couple of acres overlooking the rugged northern coast and is in the heart of Maui's rustic upcountry. The surrounding farmland is still worked by real Hawaiian cowboys called Paniolos.

I enter the main building called Hale Maluhia, or House of Peace, and I am guided to a lovely room filled with people sitting in silence. I take my shoes off and enter quietly.

It takes me a few moments to find a comfortable chair in the back amongst a few dozen people. Sitting in the front of the room facing the group is a man with his eyes closed who looks a lot like me but with glasses.

The long stretches of silence are randomly broken when he softly imparts a few wise words. His pearls of wisdom are often punctuated by a wide smile.

At some point I hear a faint chime and feel my awareness begin to slowly make its way back to the room. My Soul radically contracts to a mere fraction of its infinite Self so it can squeeze into the tiny stardust container that is known to the world as me.

When I finally open my eyes, the people are filing out behind the Sage into the bright Maui sunshine.

I then notice that while my spirit was out carousing amongst the infinite dimensions of being, an absolutely striking woman has sat down next to me. Her dirty-blond hair is tied up on her head and she is wearing black yoga pants with a loose fitting beige linen blouse.

She slowly opens her eyes and looks at me with a warm smile.

I raise my hands and slightly bow towards her, and she does the same.

She then whispers, "Wow, that was deep. I found it hard to come back."

"Me too." I look down and notice that during the meditation, I have drooled all over my tee shirt.

She notices me noticing this so I point towards my chest. "There's nothing like making a strong first impression."

She laughs and then puts her hand over her mouth. "Sorry, but that was funny."

Outside of being so lovely there is also something vaguely familiar about her.

After a little small talk we wander out through the gardens and sit by a giant statue of the Buddha across from the pool.

The girl with the very pretty face takes a long gaze and deep breath. "I love this view, and the air here is so clean and clear."

"The sweet fragrant smell of the sea." I point towards the beaches along the north shore. "A few weeks ago the waves down there were fifty to seventy feet high. It was mind-blowing."

She loosens her hair and shakes it out. "Oh, do you live here?"

"For the time being, yes. How about you?"

"I've been in Los Angeles for about ten years now."

"Oh, I'm sorry."

She smiles. "So you've spent time there?"

"Yes." I take off my sandals and let my toes sink into the soft, cool grass. "Do you like Los Angeles?"

"My family is there, and my work, but I can't say I like it. I certainly don't love it. I'm not sure anyone does."

I nod in agreement. "What's your take on the place?"

She takes a deep breath. "Well, there's a lot of ego, it's crowded, and the air is brown…"

I toss in…"And those are the good things…"

She reaches out and touches my arm. "Please tell me you're not an actor?"

"No, I'm not an actor. I guess I'm a writer. How about you? I'm guessing a model?"

She pauses for a second almost as if she is surprised I had to ask. "You are very kind. I actually started as a model, but now all the girls getting the work are about sixteen, so I'm considered ancient. Acting is my main thing. I'd love to get out of it, but I'm not sure what to do next. The money is insane, but I feel over the business."

I pause soaking up our vast vista and listen to the sound of the water in the fountain in front of us.

As we sit there and converse, I realize she is actually a pretty well known star of the small screen who has also done a lot of films, and someone who appears in the tabloids every now and again. Catching her out of context, post meditation and sans makeup, it was hard at first to place her.

Yet sitting here with the wind blowing her hair around wildly, she looks much more beautiful and natural than her red carpet movie mannequin self.

There is a nice pause in our conversation so I toss out an offer. "I think all that astral travel made me hungry. Can I buy you a little lunch?"

To my surprise, she accepts immediately. "On one condition." She holds up her pointer finger. "You let me buy."

"I see the jaded movie industry has turned you into a ruthless, scorched earth negotiator, but how about this, I'll buy lunch and you can buy dessert?"

Her look turns a bit devilish, "Do you like sweets?"

"Like is much too weak a word. It's more of a calling." I stick out my hand. "Deal?"

She shakes. "If you insist, but only if we go to a separate place after the main course."

"We must because it would be too weird to ask for a second separate check for the brownies and ice cream."

We hop in her rented SUV and head a couple of miles up the hill to Makawao, a small cowboy town with a string of shops and a nice restaurant or two. After a walk up and down the main street, we choose a charming little café with a flower-filled courtyard.

Her face and features are symmetrical and her smile comes easily, her eyes sky-blue yet laced with the traces of sorrow and sadness.

Our dark-haired waitress, whose arms are covered in tattoos, comes over to take our drink order and immediately recognizes my companion. "Oh, my. Is that really you? I love your stuff!" She then rattles off a couple of programs and film roles that meant a lot to her.

My lunch date almost seems a little embarrassed by the attention, yet is gracious in the moment. "Thank you. You are too kind."

The server says, "This must be my week of famous customers. Oprah Winfrey sat at this very table yesterday. She lives just a few miles up the street, you know, and apparently comes in a lot, though I have only seen her once."

I can't help but tease. "Oprah who? Should I know who that is?"

For a moment the waitress falls for it. "What? You don't know who..." She shakes her head and walks away.

After our server departs, I notice my lovely new friend puts on her sunglasses. It's subtle but I understand the desire for just a little more privacy and space. She takes a few moments to reboot and then asks, "So is Maui your home?"

"Not to sound too bohemian, but for the time being, yes. A couple of years ago I sold my house in Nashville and downsized to a smaller place. Then I got rid of that one and moved into an even smaller nest, all the while pruning my possessions down to a precious few.

"Eventually, I got rid of everything and hit the road. There was no grand design so to speak. My life just sort of evolved into this semi-nomadic quest of inner and outer exploration."

She unwraps her linen napkin and places it in her lap. "And you said you are an author?'

"I am..."

The waitress drops off a bottle of sparkling water at our table. I pour the Star a glass and then fill my own.

We spontaneously raise our glasses, and she says, "To new friends."

Clink...

"Aloha..." I add.

"Aloha." She flashes a lovely smile, "So you sound a little like a modern day Jack Kerouac."

I cock my head. "But minus the boozing and literary ability, though oddly enough, we both wrote about hitchhiking."

"*On the Road* is one of my all-time favorites. Tell me about your book."

A tiny sparrow lands on our table, checks us both out, but doesn't recognize my famous lunch date.

The little angel takes off and I continue. "It's called *Hitchhiking With Larry David,* and it's a true story about a magical summer I experienced in Martha's Vineyard."

She leans in. "Larry picked you up?"

"Yes. You are looking at the only person on the planet who can say that."

"That's hysterical. Does he know about the book?"

I nod. "He actually endorsed it saying, 'If I had only known, I would have been wittier.' He's been very generous."

The Star flashes her million-dollar smile. "I have to read this book. Can I get it on Amazon?"

"You can but better than that, I have a couple at my house and would love to give you a signed copy."

"Really? Well then…" She raises her glass to me and takes a long sip.

The arrival of our food breaks the flow and then the waitress fawns over the Star for a moment or two before saying, "Oh, I better let you eat before your food gets cold. Sorry."

I point out. "You handle the 'famous thing' with patience and grace."

"That's kind of you to say. I can't imagine being rude to someone who is simply reaching out and trying to connect. Most people are very respectful and gracious, but you also get your share of crazies. That part can be scary."

"I probably have no idea."

She puts a piece of seared tuna in her mouth. "Oh my god, this is so good. Please try a bite." She cuts off a piece and puts it on my plate. "What was I saying?"

"You were looking at me and saying something about your share of crazies…"

The Star perks up. "Oh yes. I've had my share of stalkers and insane paparazzi. People following you, one guy broke into my house, the tabloids going through your garbage..."

I wince. "The price of fame... by the way this tuna is amazing. Here, try some of my Mahi..." I return the favor and put a piece on her plate.

She raises a finger. "Remember, I am buying this fabulous lunch, and also your book. Writers can't be giving away their work. That's how you end up starving to death."

I put my hand on my stomach. "Do I look like I have ever missed a meal? Remember, you are in charge of dessert. I know a place on the south shore with a chocolate mousse cake where we can also catch the sunset."

I suddenly become self-conscious. "Heavens, how presumptuous of me to just assume you don't have any plans or someone fabulous waiting for you."

She finishes a bite of her entrée. "You are sweet. My day is free and there is no one back at the hotel. This whole trip is about me getting some solo space from Los Angeles and my relationship. Besides, you can't talk about giving me your book, sunsets and chocolate and then try to bail on me. That's so Hollywood."

I pretend to ponder this for a moment. "Yes, you're right. It almost makes me sound like an agent."

She leans in. "Oh, you could never be that bad."

After lunch we ride over to the south shore. I marvel at the synchronicity of meeting my lovely, famous driver and how crazy life can be if you just stay open.

My Lord, do I feel myself developing a crush on this woman? How could I not? Forget the fame. She's wonderful, fun and open. Plus she meditates and loves dessert.

Somewhere inside of me a voice says, 'Easy boy, one heartbreak at a time...' Besides, she already mentioned a boyfriend. Proceed slowly.

I place a gentle hand on her shoulder. "Not that you need me to tell you this, but you are simply wonderful."

Her mouth opens. "Ah, thank you. I have not been feeling so wonderful lately. Hey, where am I going?"

"I keep hearing about a place called Big Beach. What do you say we check that out?"

She looks at the seat behind me. "Sounds great, and I have my suit in one of those bags back there."

I glance out the window at a sparkling, clear sky. "Another perfect Maui day..."

A few minutes later we are lying on a golden beach with views for miles down the coastline. Out across the water is the tiny island of Molakai, a snorkeling paradise, and behind that, the much bigger Lanai.

She settles in on a large white towel. "This is fabulous, and look at all that bright green water. Thank you for this."

"You are welcome. Keep an eye on that aqua expanse and you might see a whale or two cruising by."

She looks out there intensely for a few moments, then up at the sun, and says almost more to herself than to me, "God, I needed this."

"Tough time?"

She lies down and turns over on her stomach. "It's been a rough couple of years."

"Care to share?"

She lets out a long exhale. "Where to start? I've been deeply involved with this very high profile man for the last five years who is married but currently separated. We have this powerful connection that makes me believe in past lives or something. I know the situation is really bad for me, but I cannot seem to break away. I came here to Maui in pursuit of clarity. The space helps, but we always seem to come back together."

"Is he in your business?"

"Yes, we met on a movie set. The whole thing is hard to explain, even to myself.

"When we met he was married, but we got involved any way. Then they separated. His kids struggled and I felt all of this guilt. Back and forth we went for a couple of years. Then he wanted an open relationship with other women, which he started to bring into our bedroom. I went with it, but it never resonated.

"There has been so much drama and I ended up getting really sick and had to go off for months and recover. My self-esteem hit rock bottom. I wondered if I was going to die, maybe a part of me wanted to."

I touch her shoulder lightly. "I'm sorry…"

She puts her head on her arms and is quiet for a while. "Thanks for listening. I probably sound pretty crazy."

I say softly, "Well, then we both are. I can relate more than you know."

She sits up. "Really? Tell me…"

"There is no fame or fortune, but the dynamics are similar though I have to confess we never had a threesome."

She playfully slaps my leg.

I look out at the water and take a few moments. "The enormous connection and chemistry, the debilitating dysfunction, the lack of logic, the moments of magic, the inner struggles… Rising like Icarus towards the sun, then crashing to the earth in a bewildering fog of mixed emotions… should I keep going?"

"I guess you do know. So what the fuck is the deal?"

Her profanity catches me off guard. "I love it that you said 'fuck!' I drop the F-bomb all the time, probably too much, and always in the worst social scenario possible. It is a lifelong affliction."

She chuckles. "Oh, I have a real potty mouth. Are you with this girl now?"

I gaze out at the horizon for a moment and watch a nice set of waves come enthusiastically ashore. "Yes and no."

I look up at the sun and then back at the Star. "She's right here on the beach with us. She's there in the bed next to me when I fall asleep, and then again when I wake up. She's on the tip of my tongue when I get good news, or when I'm broken and fall off the bike."

I shrug my shoulders. "She's a ghost I have been unable to shake. There's no explaining or understanding it. Technically she lives in Seattle with her latest 'fiancé,' but she's always with me. It all lies beyond the comprehension of my small, limited mind."

The Star, who looks magnificent on that towel, soaks this all in, as well as the infinite glow of the sun above us. "I think you nailed it. There's no logic to any of it. I wish I could simply find some peace."

Her words hang in the warm sea air and I try to wrap my mind around the concept of this woman next to me, in one sense having society's version of everything, yet nothing at all.

We lay there in stillness for a little while before she finds some sanctuary in sleep. She looks angelic with her face aglow in the soft afternoon light.

I leave her for a while and go for a long walk followed by a swim. When I return she is writing in her brown, leather journal. She looks up at me. "How is the water?"

"Not as warm as your smile. Your eyes look brighter."

"They do? I really passed out. Who says you need a pill to sleep?"

"Not me, and not here."

She marks her place and puts the journal in the bag, "Did you see any whales?"

"Just a couple on the beach over there from Nebraska."

The Star smiles, "Hey wise guy, are we still getting that dessert? Though, I shouldn't indulge, I'm already ten pounds too heavy."

I look down upon her exquisite, toned form and wonder where those ten pounds are hiding. "You have to be kidding. Your body looks perfect to me."

"I'm actually fat by Hollywood standards."

"Then move to Maui…"

She grins. "You are good for me, or a good liar. Either way I like it, and I like you."

"The feeling is mutual."

After a quick swim and a little body surfing, we ditch the beach and drive down the south coast to a cozy little place called Sarrentos. The cute hostess with long brown hair seats us at a table about forty yards from the water's edge.

The ocean has decided to mellow out and now looks like a sea of glass.

The Star takes a sip of water and gazes out at the rich tapestry of colors in front of us, her blue eyes as bright as robin eggs. "I love how expanded I feel when I look out at something so magnificent."

I nod. "Yes, the sea and the stars do it for me every time."

The waiter takes our humble order of one decadent extravagance and two forks, then recognizes her and praises a couple of films I am not familiar with.

A Maui couple I met recently at a mutual friend's dinner party spots me and wander over to our table. After first name only introductions, they mention the role my new friend is probably most famous for and their love of that show.

Once again, The Star is ever patient, kind and accommodating.

Our dish arrives and the locals depart.

I let her take the first bite before saying, "I have to admit I feel sort of foolish not immediately recognizing you. Luckily for me, God protects the simple-minded."

She puts the chocolate oozing delicacy in her mouth and she closes her eyes in ecstasy. "We may have to order one for you too…"

"Don't tell me you are also a dessert hog, and here I thought we might be perfect for each other."

She pushes the plate my way and raises an eyebrow. "We can take turns, but make sure we keep this thing civilized."

My bite explodes in my mouth. "You're right. We do need to get another one."

After savoring her next tiny piece she says, "I'm so glad you didn't know who I was, or more importantly, you didn't care. I needed that, and I needed today."

I point towards what is rapidly vanishing on the plate. "And we both needed this."

"We did. Seriously, though, thank you. You're like a guardian angel."

"Maybe I really am your angel…"

Her eyes twinkle. "So you can eat all you want and not put on a pound?"

I shake my head. "Unfortunately that is one of the many misconceptions you mortals have of the angelic realm. We always put on weight when we incarnate."

She doesn't miss a beat. "So what's another?"

"That we watch a lot of television…"

Her laughter bursts forth and the table of four sunburned tourists next to us looks our way and smiles. The Star shakes her head. "You need to come to Hollywood, kiddo."

I look at her in mock irony, "So I can be as happy as everyone else there?"

"Touché, my friend." She puts down her fork. "Look at that sky now."

I look up and see a giant orange orb hovering just above a dark blue-grey expanse of forever as an odd collection of clouds mill about like hovering attendants around royalty.

Birds come and go yet everything feels so still.

How does something 93 million miles away look so large? How can it all be so perfect?

A moment later, the great golden lady that warms our waters and grows our fields, vanishes silently into the sea.

I take a long, slow breath of oxygen and let it go but now as carbon dioxide. How funny that I rarely consider the miracle of that basic exchange that allows me to exist.

When I return my gaze to the Star she has a tear or two in those hypnotizing windows into her soul. I place my hand on top of hers and she puts her other hand on top of mine.

We dare not deface the moment with words, choosing instead to sit in silence.

The onset of night has called this day of spontaneous adventure to a close and soon we are sitting in my driveway. I invite her in for a quick tour and then reach into a tattered box and pull out a copy of *Hitchhiking With Larry David*. "Here, my friend. This is for you."

She places her hand on her heart. "You kept your promise. You keep your promises." She then puts her arms around my body and holds me tightly. "Thank you."

I hold her tightly, too.

After we let go, I place my right hand gently on her chest and say softly, "Always listen to this first and last. It's all right here."

Standing there in the soft light of my bedroom, she suddenly looks all of twelve years old, so wide-eyed, innocent, and open. "Yes." She whispers.

I look in her eyes. "Thanks for making this day so memorable."

"You too, Jack Kerouac." She suddenly has a very concerned and alarmed look on her gorgeous face. "Hey, don't you dare sell our story to any of those terrible tabloids."

I smile and shake my head. "They would never believe me."

She once again drops her guard and gives me a long sweet hug. "And you never asked to take a single picture..."

Now I put my hand on my heart. "It's all in here..."

For a moment I consider how easy it would be to fall in love with her. Yet it feels like it would only work if we moved as far away as possible from the disease of fame.

Though we make plans to meet again while she is on the island, something in me knows I will probably never see her again, except maybe in an advertisement or on some poster.

I sign the book, we hug again and I walk her out. Unspoken gratitude is exchanged as we hug some more for a little longer, and then part.

That night I fall asleep wondering if everything that happened was some kind of dream.

Who knows? Maybe it all is?

Negotiations

The next afternoon finds me in a small cove filled with bright green water and a few trees providing shade. Since no one is around, I swim in the raw and then let the sun dry the moisture from my glistening skin. The surf is calm, and I see a couple of sea turtles bobbing near the coral rocks having a little lunch.

After a few minutes of daydreaming, and then some writing in my journal, I get a text from the Star, 'Thank you for our lovely day. My boyfriend has decided to come to Maui and is arriving this evening for the weekend. I will drop you a line when I get back in the city of angels. Much aloha to you!'

As I am typing a response, my phone lights up with a call from the Broken Girl.

Flashback:

That evening without a moment's warning, she shows up at my Del Mar abode. "Pauly, I'm in a panic and have no place to go. My roommate flipped out. So I drove around awhile and then came out here."

"What happened?"

"We are months behind in the rent and she's freaking out. One of the guys I was dating was supposed to pay our landlord if I went skiing with him. But I cancelled that trip to stay in town with you."

"Wait... what... Just skiing?"

She looks at me openly. "What do you think?"

I inquire about the obvious. "What happens if the rent never comes?"

"We lose the place. But I am sick of her anyway and need to make a change. "Can I stay here a couple of days until I figure some things out?"

"Well, it's not even my house, but let me ask the owner." A few phone calls are placed and the short-term go ahead is given.

"Pauly, I am going down to the market, get some of the healthiest food I can find, and create a fabulous dinner for you."

That night with the Milky Way Galaxy as our witness, and our hearts wide open, we share a candlelight meal on the deck. Those enchanting green eyes of hers have certainly captured something inside of me. Plus I really 'like' this woman. Her circumstances are nuts, but her? Amazing!

And the hugs...

From the night we met, we began sharing these long transcendent melt-into-my-body embraces. Holding each other is an act of reunification, a time of pure oneness and neither of us can get enough of them.

Once again without even realizing it, we have talked until well past midnight. I point towards a long hallway full of empty guest rooms. "Why don't you grab one of those empty beds and in the morning, we can grab some coffee down by the beach."

She shakes her head and tears up a bit. "Thank you for being so generous and loving."

As we prepare to say goodnight and go to our separate rooms we hug again. But this time something different moves between us as well as certain body parts. She does not let me go and I can tell she can literally 'feel me.'

"Wow!" I said. "That was, ah, well, I'm sorry about that."

"Don't be sorry. I was beginning to think you weren't attracted to me and I didn't like it."

"Really? As striking as you are?"

"These days I only feel beautiful around you. But in a very different way, like you see what is best within me and love that piece of my soul. I have never felt that from another person, especially a man. It took me a while to trust it but it feels natural and supportive…Sort of freeing and unforced. Do you understand what I am trying to say?"

"I do and I do…I always seem to…"

"See I knew you would get that. You get me…"

"I feel the same way around you, understood and seen. Not crazy or strange…"

There is another hug, an awkward silence, then off we go to our separate corners of the house. After about an hour of tossing and turning, I somehow manage to fall asleep.

Sometime in the middle of the night, I awaken to her naked form pressing up against my body and touching me everywhere. She kisses my neck and then works her way down my chest.

Am I dreaming? This delicious dalliance must be a dream...

As her efforts intensify, I become fully awakened in more ways than one.

All the tension of the previous four weeks that has been building up between us is now begging to explode inside her. She grabs my hand and places it within her inner sanctum. She is soaked and warm. Her mouth caresses and teases me until I am pleading with her to finish and to take all of me.

With that she climbs on top of me, and the real fireworks begin. We go everywhere that night, both physically and emotionally.

Over the past month we have been saying I love you in a million different ways, but now we express it with our bodies.

~~~

"Hello?"

She sighs. "Pauly, my best friend Kara, the one from our healing workshop back in Nashville, has died." She begins to cry. "She overdosed on pills, and never even said goodbye to me… I spoke to her a couple of weeks ago…"

I let her cry and cry while silently wondering if she might be next.

I look out across the water and down the shore at the dark lava rock. The temperature is somewhere in the low 80s. My body still has a few beads of water on it from my swim. "I am so sorry. She was a wonderful and loyal friend to you."

"Yes… now all I have left is you…"

I resist being a wise guy and offering, 'don't forget about your live-in fiancé.'

She shares more about Kara and the last time she saw her at a wedding. How they even batted around the idea of getting a place together. Then she switches gears and asks, "Have you thought any more about me coming out there to be with you?"

I take a deep breath, and then another. "I have and wanted to bounce some thoughts off of you."

The Broken Girl gathers herself. "Please, go ahead."

I once again take in my beautiful, serene surroundings and proceed. "If you wish to come west and have me help you, there are two primary things I ask: 1) No contact with Adderall Man 2) No drugs or medications."

She pauses for a moment, then…"He is leaving for Honduras in February and will be traveling through the jungles of Central America and then Cuba, so I can easily honor your request. In fact, I think I will change my phone number so there is no way he can be an intrusion into our space. We have been sleeping in separate bedrooms for the last six months. Trust me. It is 100% over between me and him."

"I've heard that a lot over the past two years, maybe a dozen times…"

She sighs. "It's over and he's leaving. You have to trust me on this. If I wanted to be with him, I would have gone to Honduras."

"What about #2? No drugs…"

"I am not on any medication at all."

I gingerly keep proceeding. "We will sleep in separate beds, so we can enjoy each other as dear old friends."

She chuckles. "Don't you want me?"

"It's not about that. What I want is to give you a chance at a new life. When do you want to arrive?"

"Today! But I have commitments for Christmas. What if I come on the 27th?"

"You realize that is the day we met in Del Mar?"

"Pauly, how perfect!"

I am still not remotely ready to dive into all this. "Let's keep talking over the next week or so and see how this progresses. Remember, we are not getting back together. I'm offering you an opportunity to move your life in a new direction."

"Thank you, Pauly. I love you."

After hanging up and another swim, I think about bringing her to Maui and check into my gut. My insides tighten up and my breath becomes shallow.

Sitting down on a large, black lava rock my thoughts stream past me. Why even take a chance? Why mess up this peace? She is no longer my concern. Shouldn't I be selfish and stay out of her mess?

Merry Christmas

T'was the night before Christmas and my phone starts to light up with texts and pictures from her. The Broken Girl is as gorgeous as ever, but now in a sad sort of way. Her eyes look empty, absent of that wonderful mysterious sparkle I remember from our much happier days together.

After about a dozen photos I write, "You look lovely. Merry Christmas."

A few minutes later the shots become a tad more racy. Then flat-out erotic.

"Do you like your Christmas presents?" her text inquires.

I answer honestly. "Yes."

"Since Santa says you've been a good boy, there will be more to come."

Soon the videos start arriving. Most are poorly lit home movies featuring a stunningly sexy beauty in various places around the house, erotically pleasing herself or inviting the viewer to come have her.

There is one with her in a steamy shower that I could probably sell on the Internet. I feel my blood pressure rise, among other things, and my body chemistry change as I remember some of our own un-filmed carnal escapades.

Were these shorts movies perhaps a promise of what was to come if I decided to dive back into her chaotic-erotic world?

Though physically stimulating, is this what I really wanted?

In terms of the sex, the answer is a resounding yes. I have missed her as a lover. But without the context of deep, committed love, being together in physicality would take on a much more tragic tone.

Was she trying to play me? Absolutely. We both knew it. This is her game, and at one time our game, but that ship had long since sailed.

Flashback:

As a 44-year-old guy who never thought of himself as that attractive, my ego is doing back flips over this young Erotic Lottery Ticket that has fallen head first and mouth wide open in my lap.

There is only one small problem that I work overtime to ignore: Her life is a complete mess.

Unfortunately, with all of this nonstop sex, 99.9% of my Chi, or Life Force, is going out of my lower chakra. So I have about as much ambition as a retired circus lion. In other words, nothing is getting done except her.

Also my funds are taking lots of hits from what has unfolded in her life before we met. For example:

1. Oh, I thought I paid all those speeding tickets.
2. Oh, I thought I paid all those parking tickets.
3. Her Black Hole Audi is in need of constant care.
4. Medical bill collectors threatening violence.
5. Unpaid phone bills and fines so the phone can be turned back on.
6. Back car payments so they don't come and tow the Black Hole Audi.
7. Credit card debt with epic late fees.
8. A loan or two from various friends.

But...

That horrible, awful, hopeless lonely feeling (along with all my ambition) is gone!

~~~

I suddenly realize the guy behind the camera could only be Adderall Man. She is sending me films from their X-rated library!

Talk about a buzz kill...

Cousin Kathleen

As my red beach cruiser glides down the hill towards the beach, my phone receives a text.

When I reach the park along the ocean, I see the message is from my cousin Kathleen asking, 'Can I call you?'

A moment after I respond in the affirmative, the tiny device rings.

"Cousin Pauly, last night I had this amazing dream where I was with you in Maui. I lived there and the place was so magnificent and magical. Then I woke up to this frigid January morning here in Middleborough, Massachusetts and went back to feeling hopeless."

Quick Backstory

When Kathleen and I were young, we were about as compatible as a cobra and a mongoose thrown together in a small over-heated box. But as the years passed, we discovered we were way more alike then different. With time, connection and patience, a beautiful friendship began then blossomed.

Kathleen's life had taken a lot of unusual twists and turns, five maybe six or was it seven marriages (I lost count), multiple successful businesses, two grown children, losing weight, and finally finding Jesus. She even adopted her baby granddaughter, Lily, who soon became the Light of her life.

Like millions of other people, Kathleen began to run into difficulties when the economy crashed. A perfect storm of events began to adversely affect her; the new coaching business she launched didn't, her house value dropped by 70%, her car was totaled, and so on.

We had not talked in a while, so when she called with her Maui story it caught my interest. "Tell me about your dream."

She took a deep breath. "Well, first of all it felt so much more real than just a dream. With your help, Lily and I had moved there. We were both so happy. The ocean was beautiful, the breeze was blowing, and there was so much sunshine…I felt it."

"Have you ever been to Maui?"

"No, I have never been to Hawaii."

"Go on…"

"Then I woke up and for a moment or two I was still feeling that warm glow, until I realized it was the middle of January and 20 gray degrees outside. My heart sank. Nothing has been working for me lately; it's like my life is stuck. This huge house feels like a tomb. I have always been able to get something going. I'm a survivor, but this feels like quicksand." She pauses and exhales deeply. "Do you like Maui?"

I soak in the moment. "It is truly paradise, especially this part of the island. Sunny every day, warm water, golden beaches, sea turtles, healthy food…I love it."

There is a long pause. "Is it crazy for me to entertain the possibility, even the idea, I could leave everything behind, grab Lily, and move there?"

"Not at all and you would have one huge advantage."

Kathleen sighs. "What would that be?"

"Me."

"Really?"

"Oh yes. I can save you so many steps and be your human reconnaissance craft. You wouldn't have to make the mistakes I made. Things would be so much easier. I say if your heart tells you so, go for it. Remember, if you don't like it, you can always go back, or anywhere else. Then it's just a vacation or something interesting to write about later. From the sound of things, you could use a little adventure. Shit. Shake things up!"

"I'm smiling." She lets out a long breath. "And feeling that warm glow again."

"I will send you some housing links. When do you want to arrive?"

"Later today…"

This makes me chuckle. "Why don't you check on some flights…"

"What about February 1st?"

"Get busy. You can make it happen."

"Thank you Cousin Pauly."

A few days later I find an apartment just off the beach with a view of the ocean for less than fair market value. Unfortunately, there were at least 50 applications in front of her. No worries. Kathleen still gets it.

Two weeks later, I pick the two of them up and she never looks back. For days she works day and night, and with the help of the Salvation Army, turns her place into a little jewel.

With her abode feeling homey, it is time to go find her some Jesus. From a tip, Kathleen decides to check out a church in the vicinity called New Hope. (How perfect for her! But I could never get a straight answer on what happened to the old hope.)

In an effort to locate the place, she takes out a small map she had picked up for free at the gas station and, after a moment or two, her mouth flies open, her hands let go of the map and she falls to her knees in tears.

It simply could not be. It was impossible. Yet, it is said, "With God all things are possible." It was truly a miracle. It turns out she HAD been touched by Grace. She had been guided here. Thank you, God. Thank you, Jesus.

Through tear-filled eyes she looks at the map again. There in black and white, in the very spot in which she lives, were the words, *Aston Maui Vista.* Or, as one might say, Aston's Maui View...

OK.

Did I mention that my cousin's name is Kathleen Aston?

Aston! *Aston Maui Vista*

Amen...

All Kinds of Dass

As I enter the door of my favorite coffee shop, an older woman behind the counter smiles. "Good morning, Mr. Paul. Aloha." Knowing my order, she immediately begins creating the local grown brew that awakens my brain. A moment later she brings my warm latte over to me, the steam slowly rising off the top.

"Mahalo, dear one," I say, and take a slow sip.

Bliss...

A few minutes later a middle-aged man comes in, takes the seat to my left and smiles. "Good morning." He opens his laptop and takes out a pad with some writing scribbled on it. After fussing with his computer for a couple of moments, he turns to me and asks, "Do you happen to know the Wi-Fi password here?"

I break into a broad grin. "It is Aloha1111. How have you been?"

He furrows his brow and gets an intense look on his face. "Where have we met?"

"On the back porch of Morning Glory Farm in Martha's Vineyard."

"Yes! Eating salads... Oh my... The hitchhiker! Paul, what... oh my god... wait... this is crazy. What the...?" We get up and share a long hug.

I hold his shoulders. "Synchronicity strikes again! Brother Surya, what are you doing way out here in the middle of the Pacific Ocean?"

Surya Dass, which in Sanskrit means 'Servant of the Sun, is one of the leading teachers of Buddhism in the west with several best selling books like *"Awakening The Buddha Within.'* He is also extensively involved in charity work through the Dzogchen Foundation.

He steps back, "I could ask you the same thing. You look terrific. How's the Larry David book doing?"

"Selling beyond anything I could imagine. It was purchased by Gotham-Penguin and comes out in May worldwide. The whole adventure has been a wild ride."

Surya is beaming, "That is terrific and how about that beautiful girl who was with you on the Vineyard that bright, sunny day? You know, the one from the book. Is she here with you?"

Flashback:

After her post-breakup move back to Seattle, I wonder if her manner with me on the phone becomes dependent on the type of pills she has ingested. A few of the various combinations are...

- *The barely coherent, word-slurring gal.*
- *The I-haven't-slept-in-four-days-3000-words-a-minute hyper-speed chick.*
- *The sporadic, randomly-chuckling flirt with long, random pauses.*

- *The deeply emotive, sorry-for-all-the-pain I've-caused recalcitrant.*

On my side of the conversation I stay with 'completely heartbroken.' Not only did I lose the relationship, I have never seen someone I love become completely unhinged in this way.

Her whole descent feels mythological and tragic.

When I finally cut the last chord of financial assistance, she immediately jumps into a new relationship with a guy that sounds dubious at best. Also, a new pattern is established that will carry her forward.

1. Meet a new guy and immediately move in together.
2. Vanish and cease all contact with me.
3. Soon reappear and tell me about Mr. Perfect New Guy.
4. Get engaged to Mr. Perfect New Guy within a week or two.
5. Drop out of sight for about two months.
6. Return with a suddenly less rosy picture of Once Mr. Perfect.
7. Explore the possibility of reconnecting with me and trying again.
8. Disappear again for a long stretches.
9. Show up with horror stories about Once Mr. P and beg to reunite with me.

Each cycle ends with the above guy being replaced by a new ~~victim~~ man as the whole cycle starts again. It becomes sadly clear that she is simply unable to function in the world at large without a host organism.

I see so many salient signs that scream... simply stay away!

In the end, I sadly come to accept that what I once thought of as my Miracle was nothing more than my Mirage.

~~~

My mind wanders back into the present. "I'm sorry, Surya, but your question struck a chord."

"About the girl? Please tell me you two wonderful people are together."

A wave of sadness washes over me and I place my hand on my heart. "Only in spirit. No, we didn't make it."

Surya furrows his brow and his eyes reflect sadness. "Oh, I am so sorry. And I bet after you wrote so compellingly about your connection, a lot of people ask you that question."

"Oh, only forty or fifty times a week." For some reason the irony of this makes us laugh.

He shakes his head. "Life..."

"That's why I am writing the sequel, simply to answer that one question."

He hugs me again warmly. "You really loved her."

"I still do. Real love is evergreen and never dies."

The two of us sit down and order another round of java.

Our coffees arrive and Surya takes a sip from his mug. "Is she doing alright?"

I wince. "Actually she is having a very difficult time."

He puts his cup down and wipes his mouth. "What a shame. She was a sweet spirit."

My mind considers whether to share this next bit of information. "She wants to come out here and, with my help, try to rebuild her life."

He raises an eyebrow. "And?"

"I'm sitting with that one."

"Love and compassion my brother, as much for yourself as for the other."

"Do you have any advice?"

"Yes, don't drink too much coffee."

This makes me smile. His wit and intelligence are always a treat. "Boy, it's good to see you. What brings you to Maui?"

"I came to see my dear friend, Ram Dass. In fact, we are all meeting down on the beach in a couple of hours for a little meditation, fellowship and floating in the sea. Do you want to join us?"

Somebody pinch me. "Yes, of course."

After some more catching up and a bit of small talk, I leave him to his work.

A couple of hours later, I circle back to the beach and the group.

When Ram Dass arrives in an old van, they roll him out on the sand in what looks like an off-road wheel chair with giant tires.

His caretakers, a couple of young guys who stay by him constantly, and a rag tag group of old hippies then push the Guru Mobile towards the water.

A few years ago Ram suffered a severe stroke, which has left him partially paralyzed and affected his speech.

Ram Dass, born as Richard Alpert, is one of the pioneers in the western consciousness movement and an early advocate with Timothy Leery of using LSD as a means to expand one's perceptions.

Of course this sort of behavior got him fired from his prestigious teaching position at Harvard.

From there he went to India and followed the guru, Neem Karoli Baba. Ram also published the international bestseller, *Be Here Now,* which led the way for many of the modern teachers of consciousness like Eckhart Tolle and Wayne Dyer.

After we settle into a circle, sweet Surya Das introduces me to Ram Dass and then to Krishna Das, the superstar musician.

Again, for a relative newcomer, this is a whole lot of Dass. I have the inner thought that it must take a long time to rise to the level of awareness where you get the second 'S' on your Das.

While standing on the beach, a small man with a soft voice introduces himself as Gary and asks me what I do.

"I wrote a book."

The sun bounces off his sunglasses. "Please tell me about your work."

I wax on for a few minutes about the wonders of my micro-career and then ask, "How about you?"

Gary thinks for a moment and then says, "I'm retired. My wife and I live up in Oregon. We try to come out here to Maui as often as possible. Your memoir sounds interesting. I will pick up a copy. I've actually done a little hitchhiking myself."

Ram then invites all of us to go for a swim and float in a circle. He says a few beautiful blessings and mantras. It turns out his spirit is even more buoyant than the inflatables wrapped around his body.

Surya swims up next to Gary and I. "Hello gentleman, have you two met?"

Gary answers, "Yes, on the beach. Paul was telling me about his book."

Surya gives my work his seal of approval. "I read it last summer. It is fabulous. Gary, I heard Oprah is going to have you on to celebrate the 25th Anniversary of your book. Congratulations."

Me thinking: Wait… Gary… Oprah… bestseller… no wait, it can't be… no not, it has to be… retired? Then suddenly an embarrassing, sinking feeling… Gary… as in Gary Zukov… as in *Seat of the Soul* Gary Zukov… as in spiritual masterpiece… oh no… how long did I talk about my little, silly piece of writing… as in oh shit you ass…

I know sharks can smell fear, but can they smell humiliation? If so, I'm doomed.

I turn towards the tiny, floating author. "Gary Zukov?"

He smiles. "Yes…"

"Retired?"

"Yes, I am."

"Okay guys, I am just going to sink now to the bottom. Surya you can keep my scooter sitting up there in the parking lot."

Both of them laugh for a moment then Surya says, "Oh stop it."

Me looking at Gary…"Thank you for the lesson in humility. By the way, I love your books. You have made quite an impact on my life."

"You are welcome, and thank you."

I turn towards Surya. "You… not so much."

We all chuckle and Ram Dass gazes over and beams. Or was he already beaming?

This day and its unexpected unfolding is a wonderful metaphor for life.

Surya says more to Gary than to me, "I met Paul in Martha's Vineyard, and then randomly ran into him this morning at a small coffee shop.

Mr. Zukov nods. "I love it. Maybe it was not so random?"

"Amen." I say.

Eventually all of us leave the ocean and end up holding hands on the sand. We then form a circle. In a stroke of cosmic luck, Ram Dass decides to have his attendants move his chair next to me. When I go to move so one of his more enthusiastic devotees can sit close to him, he subtly motions for me to stay.

His kindness touches me.

At one point amidst all the hub-bub I happen to glance up at him in his chair, gazing serenely out at the lime green water, and I suddenly feel a deep admiration.

This man created a ripple of life force that has touched millions, who in turn affected others.

As the feeling in me expands, he suddenly turns and looks down at me. He smiles, tilts his head, then nods, while his eyes say, 'yes!' It is an utterly wordless moment where so much is expressed. I feel the sensation of tingles and my eyes well with tears. Our gaze remains unbroken. Then our hands are simultaneously guided towards each other. They meet and embrace, our eyes still fixed.

Though there is much noise and movement around us, the moment is perfectly still.

It feels as though he is giving me something, sharing… and then I hear it in my heart first, and then my head. I let it sink in slowly, my form still tingling. Then look away and close my eyes. I gaze back at him and almost silently mouth the words, 'Only Love… only love…"

He brightens a bit more, closes his eyes, nods in agreement, and then slowly lets go of my hand.

'Only Love…"

Yes, Master.

As I move through the rest of my day, I feel profoundly impacted by the magical encounter with Ram Dass and the mysterious power of unconditional love.

For some reason my mind drifts back through my inner-rolodex of people who, with no obvious or external benefit to themselves, graciously and generously helped me on countless occasions. That if not for the love of these multiple benefactors, I would not be in my privileged perch piously looking down my nose at the Broken Girl.

But for the Grace of God go I...

Suddenly I feel overcome with emotion as I remember encounters, gestures, generosity, and small acts of random kindness... given and gifted to me by an endless litany of selfless saints.

But for the Grace of God go I...

She's not my problem, he's not my problem, the world is not my problem, the homeless person is not my problem, the environment is not my problem, the endless wars are not my problem... isn't this single paradigm of disassociation the real problem?

I feel a wave of guilt for the callous way I have been listening to her cries for help...this girl, this human being in a desperate situation.

Does she have a drug problem? Obviously. Can I believe what she says? Of course not... Is she in trouble? Absolutely.

So what am I really afraid of?

I sit with that one for a few minutes.

The truth is she scares the shit out of me. I have this powerful pull towards her and it's a dangerous kind of attraction. You can't trust an addict and a compulsive liar, and even though I know this, it makes no difference. The pull is real.

Also, even though I miss aspects of what we once had, I'm doing pretty well these days. I feel good about life and have found my groove. Bringing her back feels like I am risking this tranquility for someone much more desperate than devoted.

I'm not delusional enough to think she still loves me no matter how convincing she sounds and how badly I wish it was true. But then again, what do I or really anyone know about love?

I look out across the endless sea and imagine a worst-case scenario where it is simply a disaster. Is my peace that fragile? Would I not be able to pull it all back together pretty quickly?

Yes, of course.

Again, what about her?

What if it is a catastrophe for you, but in the end it helps her? You loved this woman once, shared a life, a bed and a dream. Doesn't all of that count for something?

Especially you who have helped so many, most of them people you barely know.

What do you have left inside of you for the one who has touched you the deepest?

And really what was her crime? She loved you with all she had, gave up everything to be with you, and in the end neither of you had the capacity to make it work. Be honest with yourself here. She was struggling and you couldn't deal with it. So you let her go and sent her home, to the darkness of her parents and the patterns of the past.

Did she ever have a chance?

Is it a wonder that she ended up in a string of self-destructive relationships that only reinforced the deep-seated shame she has always carried?

Here you are living on top of the world. Can't you reach down and extend a hand to the beautiful soul who once looked upon you with such love and adoration?

If not, in the end, what is your life really about?

The tears roll down my cheeks as I sit upon an ancient lava rock and confront the capacity of my limitation.

After a few minutes I compose my self and my thoughts and call her up. "I've thought about it and I think it's best that you come. I'll do this for you. I'll give you a safe place to land, something good to eat, some time to catch your breath, a pat on the back, a chance... a chance to begin again.

You don't have to sleep with me or do anything but be clean, honest, and real. We will figure out the rest of the logistics later. You matter, and you matter to me. The world needs a healthy you."

First there is silence and then the faint sound of crying on the other end of the phone... "I don't... I..."

"I love you, and you are worth loving. Let's talk soon and figure out the rest of this. Come here and begin again. I can give you this."

"Thank you. I love you so much. I am coming home."

An Ominous Arrival

Two weeks later I call the airline to check on the status of her flight to Maui. "Sir, that flight is actually arriving 50 minutes early. They must have caught a strong tail wind."

"Thank you." I jump into my friend's borrowed car and set out to pick her up.

When I get to the airport she is nowhere to be found and is not answering her phone or responding to my texts.
In a remarkable act of kindness in the age of terrorism and fear, the policeman lets me leave my unattended-potentially-bomb laden-vehicle by the curb.

Her flight has landed. All the people from the plane have dispersed. It looks like most of the bags are claimed, but The Broken Girl is nowhere in sight.

More calls, more texts... nothing...

Then suddenly, there she is. A nice smile, and a long hug...

"Where were you? Your flight landed over an hour ago."

"My battery was dead but then it started working again. I needed to wash up and... I was going to change clothes but... I was using the restroom and I was looking for you all over... I... I..."

My heart sinks. The same old shuck and jive from the very first moment.

What surprises me is how I don't feel any pull towards her. She used to have this huge power over me; in fact, the idea of her still does, but the person? Zilch.

She definitely looks different, almost bloated, like someone has taken an air compressor and overinflated her. The long, thick hair is now darker and shorter, courtesy of what looks to be an odd hairstyle.

Though puffy, she still has that beautiful face, one that could launch a thousand ships. She looks pale and has sad eyes. A deep feeling of compassion overtakes me. "Hey you, come here." I pull her towards me. We hug again. "Aloha, welcome to Maui. You look beautiful." I whisper in her ear.

"Oh I look terrible. I've been up for days and this haircut is a disaster. My sister's friend did it after we all had too much to drink one night. Plus there was all this drama today with my parents. That is why I have not responded to any of your texts."

I nod. "Where is your bag?"

She looks sheepish. "They are over there."

"They?"

She points towards four of the largest suitcases I have ever seen, all looking like they have also been over-inflated. I know people's dogs sometimes mirror the way they look, but is this phenomenon also true with luggage?

"Didn't I say to travel *light?* There won't be enough space for all of this in my room. In fact, I am not even sure they will fit in the car."

"Well, that's all I own. I plan to stay here for good."

With the help of several hardworking Sherpas, we are able to pack, tie-down, and squeeze everything into the unattended-potentially-bomb laden-vehicle left by the curb.

As we pull away from the curb, the words are flying out of her mouth so fast that it appears she isn't taking in any oxygen. All across the island the process of photosynthesis is taking a major hit.

Her stream of consciousness... "My parents made me pack everything I own, since not even my stuff is welcome in their house anymore. Even worse, I had Adderall Man's car and then I lost his smart key. It's stuck in their driveway blocking a couple of their cars, so they are furious and can't get their own cars out. The tow truck was supposed to come but it was late, and then when the guy did... oh, did I tell you his parents changed the locks on us? They think we are druggies, I was going to break in and get my things, but then I thought... My parents, oh my god, they accused me of... What a crazy week! When Adderall Man went to Honduras his parents locked us out of their house, so I couldn't get some of the stuff I really needed for here..."

Heavens child, take a breath or two...

"Did you have any coffee on the flight?"

She misses the joke. "No, but I did take these caffeine tablets so I could stay awake the past few days and get the hell out of Seattle." Her phone is lighting up every other moment like a string of Christmas lights. "He's been calling from Honduras non-stop. He's worried about this car thing and we are trying to get a new key. It might cost $600, but if his warranty hasn't expired, it will be covered. He forgot to pay his insurance or something and it went into default. So I will need to call him or text him what's happening…and…and…"

"So in terms of you and him, it is a completely clean break?"

"Don't be judgmental like my father."

Again, this is her signature move.

"I just thought you had left him and it was over. Remember you said you were even going to change your number so he could no longer contact you?"

"Well, that was when things were really bad. We ended on good terms and we still have ties. I mean, his car is at my parent's house with some of my stuff in it. My stuff is at the house we used to live in, if we can get it out. We have a bank account. I can't just cut him off cold. I mean, he is someone I care about. But don't worry, I won't let this interfere with us."

I gesture towards her phone. "By the way, it looks like your battery recharged itself fully all by itself."

"Yes, how lucky."

We pull into my place and unload most of her cargo into the Cosmic Hoarder's already-packed garage. Once up in my room she pulls a credit card out of her pocket.

Knowing her credit history, this surprises me. "You have a Visa?"

"Oh no. This belongs to my parents. They let me use it so I could pay for all the bags. I must have *forgotten* to give it back to them."

I put a bag of her stuff in one of my closets and light a candle. "Maybe you should let them know."

She twists up her mouth in a funny way. "Do you think I should?"

"They might be worried."

She calls home. "Hi Mom. I made it.... Oh, he is wonderful... Yes, that's why I was... calling, I must have... oh... really...? Already?" She sinks and looks at me with her mouth open. "Why? OK, goodbye."

"What happened?"

"They immediately cancelled the card. What do they think I am? Man, they just hate me. I caught them telling my sister last night that they thought I was on crack or something and stealing..."

I see something in her wallet. "What's that green card?"

"Oh, that's my food card."

"What's that?"

"It's like food stamps. You use it to buy food and stuff. I've been getting these once a month for the last couple of years."

"But you were living with someone. Why did you need it?"

"Well, it's free. You might as well use it. It was my way of contributing to the household since I was living with him. He had one too."

"I thought he had a job?"

"I guess they don't check this stuff out very carefully." She catches herself and points a finger at me. "Don't judge…"

I put my hands up like I was being robbed. "No judgment here." But I am lying. "So where did he work again?"

"He worked in the psychiatric ward of a prison. It was a terrible place. There was so much darkness there, but he tried to make a difference. I really admire that about him. He was in the pharmacy and handled the inmate's different medications."

My thoughts: Oh, I see, easy access to all kinds of drugs. Drugs like maybe Adderall? So that's where they were getting all this stuff.

My words: "Wow, that takes a certain type of person to go into a place like that. I think I am a little too soft for something like that."

She tilts her head, "Are you kidding? You can't spend ten minutes anywhere you don't like. But his job was a very dark one and it definitely affected our partnership. After he began working there, things got really bad, then worse."

She takes out an Apple computer box and opens it slowly revealing a brand new Powerbook.

I take a look. "That is gorgeous. Did you just buy that?"

"No, it was my sister's but she hadn't used it yet, so I borrowed it for here. I'll need a laptop to look for a job."

Now it's my turn to grimace. "That was awfully nice of her."

The Mirage bites her lip. "Well, she has no idea. I just took it. I'm hoping she won't miss it for a while."

"Isn't she a graphic designer who builds websites?"

"Yes, but she has an older one. I do feel kind of bad because my grandfather bought this for her right before he died last year."

My mouth is hanging open and I'm already thinking it may be time to hide the silverware (as well as my checkbook). "You better send that right back in the morning..."

Her face lets me know she doesn't like my suggestion. "Well, let me think about it. Even if I keep it, my parents would just buy her another one. They favor her over me."

I put a pillow on a nice single mattress pad on the floor. "This is your bed."

She gives me a semi-provocative look and in perfectly timed fashion, takes off her tight, white pants. "But can't I sleep in the bed with you?"

The mammal in me stirs. "Remember, I promised to be a good boy and just be your friend."

"But I don't want to sleep on the floor." She purrs. "I want to sleep with you."

Believe me I would love to dive into her but I somehow hold my center. "Maybe we will get to that point again someday."

She sags but relents. "I hope I can sleep. I feel super-charged."

I blow out the candle and turn off the lamp, leaving only the beautiful glow of moonlight. A sea breeze sneaks up the hill below us and fills the room with a lovely aroma.

After a few minutes of silence, a small barely audible and fragile voice that sounds like a child floats up from the floor beneath me. "Pauly, I'm really sorry."

I turn that way and see a tiny hand cautiously making its way towards mine.

"For what, love?"

She sighs. "I'm really sorry about everything. For all of it, I'm so sorry."

"Everything?"

She lets go of another sigh. "Yes… from before… plus all the time we should have been…"

I gently squeeze her hand. "Ah, me too sweet pea, me too. We did the best we could back then."

"Pauly, I have always loved you. I love you now."
"I love you."

"Thank you for bringing me here. For saving me once again…"

"You're welcome. I am glad you are here. I'm not saving you. Sometimes we all just need a little help to get a better grip on things."

She squeezes my hand tightly and then releases it. "I love you so much."

"Good night, love. Sweet dreams."

She lets go and exhales deeply.

I look down and see her angelic face perfectly framed in moonlight, as she looks out of the window at an infinite sea of stars bearing witness to our tiny human dance.

I close my eyes and silently say a long prayer that this refugee may finally find some peace.

Day One

The next morning I hold open the door of the tiny coffee shop for her to pass through. "Pauly, how much money do you have in the bank these days?"

The directness of the question takes me completely off guard, though I have to admire the blunt approach. "You're very brave to ask me that before my first sip of espresso. Actually *any* question should wait until all three of the shots find their way into my cerebral cortex."

"Oh, Pauly. I'm sorry."

I cock my head, think about it and remember how much I like to preach the gospel of transparency. "Somewhere in the neighborhood of $70,000. You?"

The Broken Girl considers this and then smiles. "Maybe a $100, but I do have some checks I can sign over to you. That's another $600 or $700." She kisses my cheek. "You've had a good year then."

"I've been fortunate, yes. People like my book."

"Pauly, people love your book. I knew they would. I am so proud of you."

"Thank you. All of it still feels surreal."

We order our brew, and she points towards the porch. "I'll grab a table for us in the sun."

The young girl from behind the counter, with a funky haircut and lots of tattoos hands me my latte and leans in, "Is she a famous model or something?" She points towards my companion. "She's gorgeous."

I smile. "No, just someone who looks beautiful like you."

The cashier looks up and beams. "Thank you."

Maui welcomes The Broken Girl to the island with an absolutely picture perfect day. The temperature is seventy-four-humidity-free-degrees, with nary a cloud to be seen. A rather scant somewhat respectful sea breeze blows across our faces as we look across the south shore to the small island of Molokini. She takes a long sip, "Yummy. Is it always this beautiful here?"

I nod. "Day in and day out."

"Hey, I saw this car online for $3000. It is the cutest little red VW Convertible. My whole life I have wanted this kind of car. Is there any way you would cosign on the loan for me? This way I can get a reasonable interest rate. I'll pay all the payments and you can use it whenever you're here."

I point towards my cup of Joe. "Remember my whole recent First Sip Speech? Maybe let me get a little of this down, *then* ask me to buy you a car."

"Oh, shoot." She smiles. "It's just that I am so excited to start my new life." I have applied for employment online to all of the high-end resorts in an area called Wailea. Is that far from here in Kihei?"

I point towards the south. "About three or four miles straight down that road." My coffee tastes strong and smooth. "In fact the bus runs back and forth along this stretch all day. For $40 you can buy a pass that lasts a month."

"Bus? I don't want to ride the bus. Would you ride the bus?"

"I did my first week and it was a lot further than four miles. It actually wasn't bad, and I met a lot of cool people."

"But the bus..." She grimaces.

"Look, my second sip."

She smiles. "Hurry up and drink that thing."

"Hey, get a job, *then* think about the car thing."

"Is that a yes?"

"No."

"I would do it for you. Can't you help me as a friend? Would you do it if we were together?"

"Boy this third sip is really good. Going down smoothly. I feel my brain and mood brightening a bit... I'm sorry, what were you saying?"

"I'm serious. Won't you help me?"

"Of course. That's why you're sitting here."

She ups her ante. "My friends- my real friends- we would give each other our last $500. Adderall Man is like that, too. That is a big difference between the two of you. He would give me his last dollar."

"But didn't you tell me he is always broke?"

"Yes, but that is beside the point."

I consider all this for a few moments and then offer unsolicited financial advice. "Maybe he could set aside say $5000, then give you the last amount over that... this way he could still be selfless and generous, yet not have to hit up his parents all the time for money, or live in one of their houses for free."

She frowns. "That is kind of mean."

"But not inaccurate. Honest is not cruel. Hey, I guess this espresso is kicking in. Ten minutes ago that line of thinking was out of the realm of my possibilities."

"I would do it for you in a heartbeat."

"You probably would, but it is so easy to say that when you don't have to actually do anything. Not to say your intentions are not pure, but I could say right now that if I had millions of dollars, I would give it away. It costs me nothing to say it so it is as empty as the bottom of my coffee cup. Now if I had it, and wrote the check, then..."

"Never mind."

"Can we move into a lighter place on our very first morning? How did you sleep?"

"I didn't. Those caffeine pills kept me up all night. I'm exhausted."

As we converse, her phone keeps vibrating. She looks at it, reads the words, makes a face, and then puts it down. After about two dozen of these interruptions, she looks up at me and says, "I'm sorry, he won't leave me alone. He is in Central America somewhere and I guess he has Internet."

I point towards the coastline. "Walk on the beach?"

"Sure. Pauly, maybe I should try to find an apartment or even…"

I take her hand across the table. "Look, I love you and I am grateful you are here. Why don't you just take these first few days and relax. Detox, nap, eat well, meditate, exercise, and catch your breath. It's been a long and exhausting run for you."

She lets out a long exhale. "That would be great. I do feel world-weary."

"Take some time…"

"Oh, I almost forgot." She reaches into her purse. "Can we go to the bank and cash these?"

I take a look at a handful of personal checks of varying amounts made out to the Adderall Man. "What are these for?"

"Do you really want to know?"

"If I am going to put my name and money into it, yes."

"He sells Adderall to his friends and other people for $10 a pill. Believe me. It adds up."

Uh-oh.

Why am I even surprised? "You know, that is illegal? I knew a guy in Nashville who went to jail for a year as a result of something like this. Aren't you afraid?"

"No, should I be? What's wrong with it?"

"Didn't you say he is addicted to the stuff?"

She shakes her head. "He was but not anymore. He quit in Honduras. He's been down there eating healthy and juicing. He sounds great on the phone and looks much better in the pictures, too."

I deadpan. "So you really did cut him off cold and completely?"

She laughs out loud. "Don't worry… It's just that we have to work out the whole lost car key thing and figure out these checks, plus our bank account money."

"You still have an account together?"

"Yes, and half of the $3000 dollars in there is mine."

"Didn't you tell me more than once he has trouble holding on to his money? Maybe you should play it safe and get your half out now."

"He is a crazy spender, but he promised not to spend my part."

I nod. "OK..."

"So, will you cash these checks?"

"Let me think about it..."

When we return after our breakfast and walk, there is a FedEx package leaning against my door.

I pick up the box and open it. "Look at this." It is the first hardcover copies of my book, *Hitchhiking With Larry David*. I hand one to her.

"This looks amazing." She is beaming. "I guess I never told you, but I used to pick this up while we were apart and read some of the sections just to feel closer to you. During my tough times it helped remind me of us in better days."

This surprises me. "I had no idea."

"When I was in some of my darkest spots it lifted me up and it was a way to still feel connected to you." She holds up the book. "This book is you... in print form."

Her words mean a lot to me, more than I realize.

She holds the book closely to her chest. "Pauly, I am just so proud of you. Do you realize what you have done here? You wrote an amazing book that really touches people. Wait until the world discovers this." She holds it over her head. "Wait until the world discovers you! Your life will never be the same."

"You really think so?"

"I know so. My secret dream is that you will let me come along for the ride. I want to be a witness."

"Well, it's not a secret anymore…"

She thumbs through the pages, pauses, and then says, "The Miracle will live on forever in these words."

I point towards my chest, "And in here…"

"Oh my God, that is so moving." She begins to cry. "I'm sorry. I didn't mean to rain on the celebration."

I hold her for a long time. "I think it's appropriate that you were here when I opened that box."

In the intimacy of this moment, I can already sense a certain gravity building between us. I give her a long hug. "I'm really glad you are here. It's been nice to reconnect."

She holds me tightly. "Thank you. I feel it, too." Then, still holding one of the galleys, "Can I keep this one as a memento and will you sign it?"

"Of course."

The rest of the day blows by us as we spend our time catching up and filling in some of the large, missing gaps of time. Every couple hours she has to step away and deal with Adderall Man, who literally never stops texting.

That night she once again inquires if she can make the move into my bed, and though I consider it for a few moments, I decide it is still much better to keep things pleasantly platonic.

Day Two

We lay silently in the shade of a few old sea pines, just a couple yards from the ocean's edge. The hypnotic sound of the water has put me into a wonderfully altered state. I open my eyes to see the wind pushing puffy white cumulus clouds across the radiant face of the sun.

She touches my hand. "How do you feel?"

"Heavenly."

Two little boys run by us in their bathing trunks and scream in joy as they dive into the welcoming waves.

She watches them and says, "The sweet sound of joy." She turns her head towards me and I towards her.

After arriving from Seattle sans sparkle, she is beginning to sparkle again. We are just inches apart and I behold in her green eyes a renewed glow.

A gentle breeze passes over us.

Looking into her, my mind drifts back over a tattered landscape of fractured intimacy.

Though a little run down, she is still a striking woman.

I used to wonder how I ended up with this stunning female? Me: the drifter, wanderer, loner, who wished not for material things and kept so many at arms length.

I close my eyes and feel my breathing align with the cadence of the cascading waves.

Her whisper interrupts my reverie. "Did you fall back asleep?"

"No, I was thinking about how lovely you are."

"Ah Pauly, I have always felt seen around you. You are the only one who has ever got me."

"You're kind, but I'm not sure how anyone could miss it."

"You would be surprised." She lets out a long exhale and suddenly winces with pain as her hand instinctively reaches down to the lower part of her abdomen.

I quickly lean up, "Are you ok?"

"My body has not fully recovered from the procedure." She turns her head away from me and towards the water's edge.

I notice a scar that was not there during our time together. "They left a nasty mark on you."

"I had an ectopic pregnancy that went bad, and I…" Her voice trails off into the sand.

I place my hand on her shoulder and squeeze her slightly.

"Oh, Pauly…"

We lay there in silence for a while.

I hear her whisper, "I am obviously trying to fill some huge inner hole. Emotionally, it's all too painful. I sometimes wonder what has become of me."

A great wave of sadness washes over me.

As much as I would love to avoid any responsibility for the state of her life, a part of me knows this involves me. I plucked her out of her chaotic Southern California life and thus took on an emotional stake.

She gave me some of her best years with dreams of building a life together and having children.

Was this a healthy choice? In retrospect no, but it is what it is. I also sent her back to her parents, which only accelerated her downward descent.

Would we have still been a disaster if we had stayed together?

That is a mystery that will forever remain unsolved.

For a moment I feel I might burst into tears, but the feeling of sorrow passes.

I feel haunted by the fact that it just feels too late for us. Too much damage has been done, and a deep layer of scar tissue has formed around us. Could we ever resuscitate, recover and reclaim the beautiful bubble of love that grew out of our Del Mar unification?

As the children play in the water, she breaks me out of my mournful journey down memory lane. "Pauly, are you still of the mindset that you never want to have children?"

I pause and remember…

Back in the days of our shared happiness, this was one of our deal breakers.

Unfortunately, for a guy who had just sold his business and was moving as rapidly as possible toward a kind of scorched earth simplicity, her maternal desires, if embraced, were a form of material heresy.

Babies, mommies, houses and what not all require a healthy cash flow, usually dependent upon a hardworking dad, a role at that time I wanted no part of.

I reach out and squeeze her hand. "Over the past year, I have had a shift around this."

This catches her attention and she turns my way.

"After all of this endless traveling and exploring, I suddenly realized the only thing that matters are people, and none more than your wife and children."

She looks surprised. "You really feel that way?"

"It's obviously not simple, and it appears to be anything but easy, yet what else matters in the end as we take our last breaths? What we achieved, or who and how we loved?"

"No more wandering?"

"I'm re-engaging in the world with this book. I need to discover avenues that will create the financial infrastructure to support a family. Love is essential, but you need income to pay the rent and buy diapers."

"You felt so different back in Del Mar."

"If this guy went back in time now," pointing towards my own chest, "to that miraculous night when you walked in with your golden blond hair and sad eyes, the outcome would be completely different."

She bites her lip. "You have to wonder…"

"What is sad is that I let the 'idea' of what I believed to be what I wanted override the feeling. Mind over heart, I will never do that again."

She looks out over the lime green waters and the boys body-surfing in the waves. "I'm trying to conceive of what that kind of us might have looked like."

"You know, so much depends on timing. When we met, I was on my way out of the working world. I was done building a career or chasing the dollar. Remember I was selling the house, releasing everything, and planned to travel the world with a small bag."

"Then?"

"I met you that night in Del Mar. We immediately shared something, and it quickly grew into the most beautiful thing imaginable."

She smiles. "Even before that first kiss."

"Yes…" I reminisce for a moment and then regain my train of thought. "So you showed up and I thought 'holy shit!' If I jump into this, it is a whole new game. I would have to reverse my course completely and, heaven forbid, alter my plan."

She hands me the bottle of water. "You were honest with me from day one."

"Yes, I was. But I loved you madly."

She turns away and a single tear is finds its way down her right cheek.

I reach out and touch her arm. "I'm sorry."

For a few moments she says nothing. Then, "This trip is healing some very old wounds."

The sun is shining on her olive skin and radiating on that beautiful face. "It's been a long time since I felt happiness. It's been the darkest time for me." She exhales deeply.

The moment is sublime.

She leans over and gives me a warm kiss on my cheek. "Thank you, Pauly."

I reach up and gently touch her face. "I'm so glad you're here."

That evening before dinner, we stroll up from the ocean walkway to an area full of high-end retail shops.

"Oh look, a Tiffany's and tomorrow is my birthday. Can we go in, just to take a look? Please?"

I cock my head. "I'm not sure it is ever safe to take you shopping."

She smiles devilishly. "You do have a good memory."

Nothing lights up The Broken Girl like expensive jewelry. Coming from a long line of retail queens, she was born and bred to shop. In fact, she is literally incapable of saying the word 'budget.' I always felt she needed some insanely rich guy capable of making more money than she could ever spend. (If that was even possible.)

So it surprised me that, though she sometimes dated wealthy dudes, she mostly gravitated towards dead beats like myself.

We enter the store and with a supernatural sixth sense she walks towards the glass display with the largest stones. I have to admit that, as long as my credit card stays safely in its holster, I get a real kick out of the whole thing.

"Oh my, look at that one." She points. The eager salesgirl's eyes widen.

The salesgirl places a ring on her finger. This is an 11-karat masterpiece. The Broken Girl has a strange look, and I am immediately reminded of Gollum's eyes near the end of the film, *The Lord of the Rings.* 'My Precious!'

Feigning excitement to fit in I ask. "That's striking. How much is it?"

The salesgirl looks at the tag. "This one is $840,000… plus tax."

Okay, play it cool. I think she just said $800 grand for a small rock. Don't blanch or anything. Did she really say $800,000? There's no way a… holy shit, wasn't that nice condo on the hill with a view of the ocean $600,000? This rock costs more than a home with a water view? How did they ever convince people to literally buy into this? Wait, they're talking. I better get back there mentally and pretend that this is a perfectly acceptable price.

My lovely companion then informs me. "She was just saying you would definitely want to insure a ring like this. Do you like it?"

I take her hand and look more closely. Me thinking: 'It looks like a small, clear stone.' Me saying: "It is dazzling like you."

She smiles and holds out her hand. "This definitely says to the world I'm 100% taken."

"So would a full length Burqa." I quip.

The eager-to-please salesgirl sensing an epic commission asks, "What's a Burqa?"

I lean towards the counter and whisper. "Those head-to-toe black beekeeper suits some Muslim women are forced to wear."

"Are you two Muslim?"

Okay, that joke completely missed. "No, not anymore."

My girl points at a much smaller ring. "How about this one?"

The suddenly less-than-eager salesgirl sags a bit. "This is a 4-carat Princess cut."

It certainly looks modest in relation to The Goliath Diamond.

The salesgirl adds, "This one is about $200,000."

I jump in. "Plus tax."

My bachelor-trained mind starts doing all kinds of interesting calculations: How many years in Thailand would that be worth? How many massages? How many winters in Maui? How many seat upgrades when traveling? How many second-hand shirts?

$200,000 = 5 years in Maui with a weekly 90-minute massage.

$200,000 = 12 years in Thailand with a daily 90-minute massage.

My mind drifts back to the $800,000 stone. What about that one? How could something that weighed less than eight ounces have that kind of value?

My lovely partner asks, "Are you all right?"

"Yes, I was just thinking about the ring."

She gets a sly look. "Are you 'thinking about the ring,' as in maybe surprising me with it?"

"Anything is possible…" Hey, nothing like tossing out a vague, esoteric truth to get a guy out of a tight corner.

She places those lush and soft lips against my freshly-shaved cheek and gives me a moist little kiss. "I would love to someday wear your ring."

Me thinking: 'Do you mind if it's cubic zirconia?'

Me saying: "How romantic…"

But paying someone $200,000 for a silly little rock out of the ground? This felt like a terrible con and almost as bad as what religions can do to people. $200,000? That's 200 motor scooters…

Her soft voice pulls me out of my mathematical bachelor trance. "Are you hungry?"

"Yes, very. Since we are already in the high-end rent district, how about a little sushi over at the Four Seasons? It is close enough for us to walk from here."

She takes my arm. "Pauly, you are so spoiling me."

$800,000 for a small piece of the earth! If civilization collapsed it would literally be worthless. I mean, what is water going to be worth when there is not enough of it?

I turn towards her and lean in. "$800,000 would buy a lot of sushi."

She looks at me quite earnestly. "Trust me when I say in the next five years you are going to be so rich."

"Funny, I already feel that way." And I wasn't kidding.

Over at the resort we sit on large soft chairs and take our time with a fabulous meal. With her burgeoning tan, she looks quite resplendent in white. "Pauly, we can have this life. We can have it all. I am so grateful you brought me here."

I lean over and give her a soft kiss on the hand. "What a beautiful day and magical night." I raise my glass of Perrier. "To the new you."

She suddenly looks very sad.

I lean in. "Oh, I'm sorry if I…"

"Oh love, it's not what you said. I just wish we had never split up and had already started a family. That in this moment we were here on vacation together, or better yet, had a home here. Wouldn't that be perfect?"

I give her a sly grin. "I love the idea of Mom and Dad getting away for a nice dinner on date night."

After we finish, I go to the men's room and end up standing at a urinal to the right of Steven Tyler, the lead singer of Aerosmith. Hovering to his left is some kind of strange guy pitching him an idea as we both take a leak. Steven looks at me and all I can do is chuckle and shake my head. Eventually the guy gives up and leaves.

Standing at the vanity a moment later, washing our hands in separate sinks, I say, "Well, I guess after all of these years, a guy like you must get used to stuff like that."

Steven raises an eyebrow and jokes. "You NEVER get used to that. I mean dude, I'm taking a wiz!"

"Well, give him credit. Talk about a captive audience."

Tyler shakes his head and then throws up his hands. "Geez."

As we walk out together Steven sings the praises of Maui life and the importance of healthy living. I introduce him to my gal and he is gracious.

Steven departs and I open my palms to the heavens. "What a night! Rock stars and..." Then pointing towards her, "Superstars."

She smiles and hugs me so tightly. "My Pauly. Only you could go to the bathroom and end up meeting someone famous."

Day Three

We wind our way along the coast on the scooter with her arms clinging tightly to my waist, her chin leaning on my shoulder. We stop for a couple of lattes beside the ocean as the palm trees sway on a cloudless morning.

"Pauly, this is perfect. I remember how you always made my birthdays so special."

"Well, it is a pretty big deal for a soul to go to all the trouble of creating a form and may I say your body is a magnificent creation."

"I forgot what's like to have someone be kind. It's so healing!"

The view is spectacular and there are whales in the near distance breeching. I point towards the giants. "I would give anything to get close to them someday. Even from here they feel so magical."

She nods. "I think it would be wonderful to go snorkeling together."

"Yes, and speaking of wonderful, In ninety minutes you have a massage scheduled with a local woman who has healing hands."

She opens her mouth wide like a four-year-old girl. "You are indulging me. Maybe I need to spoil you back?"

"You already are by just being here." I give her a gentle hug. "Then you are getting those nails done. You have chewed them all to bone."

"I can be a worrier."

I wind my way back and drop her off. I watch her vanish into the spa.

Three hours later we are back on the scooter as we ride out past the resorts to the lava fields of La Perouse. We pull over and find a tiny cove filled with green water. We swim for over an hour and then fall asleep on an old sheet nestled in the sand beneath a grove of palm trees.

Once again her phone keeps going off, but this time she shuts it down and puts it away in her bag. "I'll deal with him later, or maybe even tomorrow."

On the way home we spontaneously stop and pick up some red roses for the room.

"Pauly, do you remember in Del Mar when you handed me roses through a window on my birthday and I burst into tears?"

"There was a light mist and a rainbow in the distance."

She gets a really far-off look in her eyes. "That was such a magical time."

"Yes my dear, as enchanting as that rainbow."

That evening, on her 36th birthday, I grant her wish and take her to the Grand Wailea resort for dinner.

As we enter the giant atrium she whispers, "My parents brought me here as a child." My date looks stunning in a floor-length aqua blue dress.

She squeezes my hand. "It's so nice to wear high heels again. My ex is a bit of a shrimp, so I always felt like an Amazon." We come upon what looks like a giant fake lagoon. "My sister and brother would go down that very water slide. I love this hotel."

I soak up the scene. The Grand reminds me of Walt Disney's *idea* of Hawaii with endless pools, faux Tiki-bars, transplanted palms, and most importantly, scores of overweight, pasty white people decked out in Hawaiian shirts.

The prices are also Disney-like.

We settle into a table at their oceanfront café, where the smell of the sea permeates your being.

Sitting next to her, I lean in. "It is neither hot nor cold, and if we don't say anything we can hear the waves gently kissing the shoreline. Does this suit your tastes, my exquisite friend?"

"This is easily my best birthday ever. I can't remember being this happy in years.

Pauly, I so appreciate you keeping in touch with me. Your random texts, inspiring words, affirming compliments, and just knowing you were out there kept me going. Did you miss me?"

"I did, quite often in fact. It was hard when you would randomly vanish for long stretches. I worried about you."

"Those were my hardest times. I only wanted to call you when I felt like I had something positive to say. Or at the very least some spark, some hope."

"Really? I thought you only called when you were down."

"Actually, it was the opposite."

I pause to consider this. Another assumption bites the dust. I guess I need to reread *The Four Agreements* or better yet, start living from that place. "I had no idea."

"There is a lot you don't know. But the thing is we have time now to catch up. There is so much I feel led to share with you. That I believe will help you, heal you, and hopefully grow you. That's why I came. I want to help you. I love you. This time here in Maui is a gift and we must embrace it."

Her supportive words warm my being. "I am always a work in progress."

The waiter comes and clears away our salad plates.

She reaches across the table and takes my hand. "I could always feel you, even in the years we were apart. Even when I was in love with someone else, it never mattered. You were right there with me. I still feel you. It is almost like we are the same soul."

"I feel like I owe you an apology."

"For what? This has been the best birthday ever: roses, a massage..." She holds up her hands. "Getting my nails done, snorkeling, the sunset, this dinner... what could you possibly be sorry about?"

"Only all the important stuff." I take a long deep breath and let it all go slowly. "Years ago you gave me your soul on a silver platter, and in my ignorance and pain, I threw it back at you. I don't have many regrets in this magical life of mine, but what happened with you has to be near the top of the list."

She reaches across the table. "Pauly..."

"Oh girl, no one has ever loved me like that. I want to go back in time and say to that guy, "Love like this does not come along very often, if ever. Treat it like the precious gift that it is. Be careful with it, for once it is broken, it can never be put back together."

She is looking at me with her mouth open like a deer caught in the headlights.

Over the flickering candle, I continue, "You left everything and everyone for me. You put all of your eggs in my basket, and I acted like a selfish, self-absorbed brat. It is such a tragedy because the entity that is us is now covered with so much scar tissue... and there is no way to go back to that level of mutual trust."

She is holding my hands tightly. "I love you so much…"

"I don't deserve your forgiveness, but here on your birthday, I can tell you how deeply sorry I am. I have not only had to live with these realizations and the regret, but even worse, I have had to live without you."

"I have already forgiven you a thousand times. I always did, and I always will. That is what love is."

Day Four

"Wake up, sweet Pauly. Do you want to go get some coffee?"

"Absolutely. I need to get those three sips into me."

She kisses me on the forehead. "Why don't we take the scooter out to Wailea, get some coffee at one of the resorts, then sit on a bench in front of the beach and drink it."

I soak in some soft sunlight through the window. "Excellent idea."

After a short scooter ride we arrive by the sea. The green water is choppy and the temperature of the air is about 70 degrees. We grab two tall lattes and sit in our favorite spot.

"Pauly, when do you have to be in Los Angeles?"

I take a long sip as a couple of wild parrots land in the tree above us. "No later than the middle of March."

She looks startled. "That's only four weeks from now. What will I do without you?"

"Do you definitely want to stay in Maui?"

"I do. Plus, I can't go back. All those bridges have been burned." She suddenly looks anxious and takes out her phone for no reason, then puts it back in her purse.

"Pauly, maybe I should walk up to the resorts after we drink these and pick up a few applications?"

She takes a long sip of coffee. "Speaking of ideas, I've been thinking, what if you rent an apartment for the two of us here in Kihei and then come back when you've finished promoting your book?

"I could also get a car for us to use. There was one online for about 17K that looked really cute.

"We could make a new commitment to each other and see one another as often as possible.

"As I have said for years, you need to live primarily in Los Angeles and get involved in the film business. I could even come there sometimes and see you."

Me thinking: So I would rent a place here and also in Los Angeles on top of buying a car for here while helping you get on your feet?

Me saying: "You realize I have to be in LA for at least three months then back East for about four months, so I wouldn't be able to return to Maui for a pretty long time?"

She goes on. "It would be our new beginning." She leans in. "We could make it work. I'll get a job and pay the bills on this end. Maybe I can even come see you back East?"

Me thinking: Monetarily this plan is a disaster. I don't really need to rent anything for at least six months while I roam around in promo mode. Oh yes, and a car? She would need insurance and gas money. This is insane.

Me saying: Let me think about this for a while. I appreciate you putting so much energy into these ideas.

"I saw a couple of places online that were perfect for about $2400 a month. There was one nice two-bedroom with a water view that I loved."

"Water view, two bedrooms?"

She gets a text. "Oh shit, they are going to shut off my phone. He must have forgotten to pay my bill."

"I'm sorry. What did you say?"

"Adderall Man was supposed to pay my bill and didn't. I need to give them $400 dollars by the end of the week or they will shut it off. Can you help me?"

"What about using some of your mutual bank account?"

She gets a frowny face but says, "I guess I could, but that was going to be living money."

"Well, a phone bill is definitely a part of living."

We wander back up through the resort and over to the high-end shops. She picks up about a dozen applications, before spotting Tiffany's.

Detour!

"You're back!" The Tiffany's girl exclaims.

Possible salesgirl thoughts: Perhaps there is a huge commission headed my way? One can dream, right? Didn't P.T. Barnum once say, "There is a sucker born every minute?" Maybe she worked all night to convince him? Let's hope so. This check couldn't come at a better time. I can get those crazy-looking, overpriced shoes I've had my eyes on forever, maybe hair extensions, a new tattoo, and if anything is left over, catch up on my delinquent car payments!

I slowly take out my wallet and offer, "We have decided to get the big diamond."

The salesgirl's eyes become much larger than the actual insanely-priced rock.

My companion hits my arm. "Don't listen to him. He's just messing with you."

As the color drains from her face, our Tiffany's girl sinks like one of those Macy's Day Parade floats that suddenly sprung a huge leak.

I feel badly but still add, "We were going to get it, but last night ended up watching the movie, *Blood Diamond*, and it just killed the whole vibe for us."

The Broken Girl gives me a look but has more important fish to fry. "Can we see this one?"

With all the energy of an old dog awakened from a long nap, the salesgirl opens the display case and takes out a small, simple, shiny, silver ring. "Here..."

I cut to the chase. "How much is this one?"

With eyes a bit downcast our counter girl says, "That one is $350."

Once again I can't help but add, "Plus tax..."

Salesgirl thoughts: Let's see here, we went from a ring in the neighborhood of $900,000 to one under $400. What percentage are we talking here... or quite sadly, 'there will be no new tattoo.' FUCK!!!!

My partner is unfazed, instead looking at her recently manicured hand with the simple ring. Like most of modern America, she really likes bright shiny things. "I love it. I had one just like it, but it was lost."

Did I mention my little gal has a way of losing things? In fact everything I ever bought her, gave her, loaned her, whatever, she lost: A couple of iPhones, an expensive watch, rings, earrings, clothes, sunglasses, jewelry, affection... in the end it was always lost.

It suddenly strikes me that she is replacing a similar gift from another guy. "Are you running some sort of Ex-boyfriend Zero Dollar Deductible where the latest victim pays to replace the lost treasures of the previous suckers?"

My sardonic comment doesn't break her trance. "No, not at all. I just always loved this ring and was heartbroken when I lost it."

"May I ask how many boyfriends ago was this initial ring given?"

She thinks for a moment, "Three… No two…"

I do the math, rummage through her rogue's gallery and ask, "Was that the guy who put a gun to your head in Spokane?"

Tiffany's Girl looks up with her mouth open and then tactfully puts her head back down.

Salesgirl thoughts: WTF, a loaded gun? And these two looked normal…

While continuing to stare at her hand, she says, "Pauly, how do you remember things like that?" She momentarily gives me an unhappy frown. "But yes, that was him. He used to love to spend every penny he had on me. Especially on gifts, which you know is my love language."

"I thought money was your love language?"

Tiffany's Girl laughs out loud at that one.

I immediately envision a two-column spreadsheet on her past boyfriend with 'likes to buy me gifts' on the plus side, 'likes to point loaded weapons at my head' on the negative side. Since they were together for almost a year, I can only imagine that in her world, these two qualities must cancel each other out.

"You know I love gifts." She holds up her hand with the ring. "Do you like it?"

"It's simple..."

"And a lot more affordable..."

Her phone continues to vibrate. Once again she looks at it, makes a face, then turns it off.

Her thinking: Hey buddy, I'm trying to close this deal here...

I reach over and take her hand for a moment. "It still feels weird to replace a ring from another guy since we are just friends, and your current ex is still calling every two minutes. I guess we could ask The Adderall Man to buy the ring, and you know he would, but he's probably broke..."

"Forget all that. Just buy it for me because it makes me happy. It can be my birthday present."

The part of my brain that gives gifts to people who lack appreciation does a brief inventory of recently appropriated items to this one particular life form.

1. Free trip to Maui
2. Free lodging in Maui
3. Free food in Maui
4. Free massage
5. Free manicure

6. Free roses
7. Three free elegant dinners
8. Free new backpack

And for heavens sake, we had only been together for a couple of days...

Another part of my brain, the part that processes requests for financial assistance from people who feel pathologically entitled submits a companion list related to this particular life form.

1. Co-sign for a $3000 car
2. Co-sign for a $17,000 car
3. Sign a lease for a $2400 apartment
4. Pay the deposit and rent for an apartment $4800
5. Pay $400 for an overdue cell phone bill
6. Give her $$$ money to get started

And once again, we had only been together for a couple of days...

She breaks me from my inner calculations. "Can I get it?' She looks so excited. "Please?"

Was I feeling morning sickness or perhaps a blood sugar crisis? I definitely am a bit light-headed. "I need to think about it. I'm feeling a bit overwhelmed."

This girl is obviously off her usual A+ game.

Speaking from my past experience, her usual plan is to ply you with a couple of months of the most incredible sex you will ever experience. Then once you are firmly in her grasp and under her spell, the requests start to drift in. You will see a bill pop up, a debt to repay, some clothes she wants, maybe a new car, and so on. I mean so far she hasn't seduced me once and we are almost up to $50,000 in requests.

It crosses my mind that she seems to be in a hurry, but why?

We still have a couple of weeks ahead of us, so I don't get it.

I silently start to wonder how long I can last around her. Though pleasant, there is something draining happening, and it is not just the countless requests for assistance. If anything it feels more energetic.

A healer I once knew told me that people with addictions are similar to vampires, but it is only energy, not blood they suck. Is this the case here?

She reluctantly gives the salesgirl the bright shiny thing back and we leave.

Two hours later we are sitting outside my favorite juice bar watching an endless array of hippies come and go.

Over a couple of large green smoothies she says, "I feel like my body is slowly detoxing from all the chemicals in those horrible pills."

She takes a nice long sip and looks out at the water. "And to see the sun again, it feels like it has rained the past four years in Seattle. I'm so glad that dark chapter is over." She lets the sun's rays soak on to her face.

Our juices sit on a simple picnic table with a hundred-million-dollar view. A tiny brown sparrow lands between the bottles, considered us for a moment, realizes there is nothing to eat and flies off.

The Broken Girl leans over and kisses my cheek. "Thank you for this."

She takes another sip. "This stuff is fantastic." A long pause, a deep breath or two, "When I think of some of the decisions I made, the choices, the mistakes, all of it was definitely affected by the medications. I would never date some of those guys or do whatever…"

Her phone keeps buzzing. She looks at it. "He won't stop texting and calling. What should I do?"

"Turn the ringer off, ignore him, change the number. Hell, move to India…"

She chuckles. "I guess I could." She flips the switch to silent.

"Thanks. It's been intrusive."

"I'm sorry. I feel at a loss on how to deal with him."

I take a long sip. "Back to the pills…how did you start taking that stuff?"

She looks off in the distance and then down. "When the two of us broke up and I went home to live with my parents, my life just completely crashed. Some days I was so depressed I couldn't get out of bed. Part of me didn't want to live anymore."

"I had no idea…"

"Well, I didn't tell you. As tough as things got with us, even at the end, I was still madly in love with you and thinking we were going to spend our lives together…"

I look her straight in the eye. "If only to keep fighting…"

She laughs and almost spits out her juice. "Yes. But truly, when it really sank in that we were over, I just dissolved. I loved our life, and then it was gone. I felt this overwhelming feeling of utter hopelessness. My Mom, God bless her, took me to the doctor and he put me on an anti-depressant."

"Did it help?"

"At first, it did. They don't make you happy, but you're not as sad either. You become sort of numb. I was sort of listless, so they put me on Adderall to help me focus."

I lean in. "What was that like?"

"Like drinking a couple of gallons of espresso."

"And…"

"The problem is the combination of the different medications gave me these terrible headaches so then they prescribed these powerful pain killers that cured the headaches, but completely knocked me on my ass. I'd lay in bed all day, so in an odd way I was back to square one."

"But with all that chemical shit in your system…"

"And it messes with your mind, literally. You have no idea. I mean, I know you won't even take an aspirin."

"True. Pills scare me."

She looks at me with sad eyes. "They took me to a very dark place and you can't just jump off of them. Once they are in your system…" She shakes her head. "Then I hooked up with my old high school boyfriend who was into some pretty bad stuff."

"Drugs?"

"Nothing hard really, well maybe some, and drinking, running with a bad crowd, but with these medications in my body, I actually felt drawn to this life. Growing up so insanely Christian and completely controlled, it was like exploring my dark side. There was a strong element of rebellion in it for me."

"Can you share some of what happened?"

She bites her lip. "Do you really want to know?"

"Why not? It's part of your path."

"We went to sex clubs, S & M clubs, took drugs, drank, there were loaded guns…"

I feel my stomach tighten up. "Did you like all that?"

"Honestly? I liked the sex clubs. It was exciting and weird too. Having sex in front of strangers. I didn't like the torture stuff-hurting someone else-that felt wrong."

This was such foreign territory for me. It was like sitting with a traveler who had visited exotic places I had not seen, not that any of it called to me. "I guess our life together was quite tame by comparison."

"Oh yes..." She gently touches my arm. "We had great married sex, and a lot of it, but you know it's fun to mix it up."

"I'm sure the Cosmic Hoarder has a whip or two in one of those boxes of hers. I'd be more than happy to tie you up later."

She smiles... "Funny. But seriously, maybe I need to be in an open relationship?"

"I guess it depends on the mutual goal. If it is intimacy you're after, then that wouldn't work, but if it's erotic adventures, distraction and stimulation, then that would be the way to go. As long as the kids don't find out..."

"Very clever... I went to some of these same clubs with Adderall Man too. He liked it. That is where he is better for me than you. He's very open to anything and I can do whatever I choose. Though we did get in an awful fight one night at the club, but that was probably due to all the hard alcohol we had."

"What happened?"

"You're really okay hearing all this?"

"We're just friends."

"He was paying too much attention to this one girl and I asked him not to. But he still did, so I got with this guy and he freaked out and just left me there. I ended up wandering around this really scary area of Seattle in the middle of the night until dawn. Then he locked me out of the house."

"You're right. All of that does sound exciting and fun."

"Don't be sarcastic..."

"I'm sorry. Sometimes I can't help myself. I wasn't judging, though..."

"He got over it, I guess we did. Hey, every couple has their stuff."

Thinking... really?

I nod. "This is true."

"The thing is, I'm not sure I would have done any of this stuff if I wasn't hooked on all these pills. Later, I found out that you are never supposed to mix what I had been prescribed. That is probably why I lost all that weight and was bleeding all the time."

I finish off the last of my juice. "Is that when you called me because you were convinced you were dying of cancer?"

She shakes her head. "Yes…"

I turn much more somber. "I believe those pills are designed to be addictive, just like cigarettes. It's good for business. Boy, you have been on quite a ride."

"Now that I am here I just want to detox and clean out." She takes out her phone and it immediately lights up with a bunch of texts from Adderall Man. She reads them, types some words back, and asks, "He needs to talk. Do you mind if I call him?"

Of course, this ongoing dialogue and drama is in violation of what had been asked and agreed upon before visiting. But even if I said no, I knew she would just slip away and do it anyway. "Sure, go ahead. I think I'm going to go to the gym."

She studies my face. "You're upset."

"Honestly, it's more a mixture of shock and awe, with a little confusion."

I realize she seems kind of dark and there are aspects of me that are drawn to her, so maybe that is something that lies within all of us. Perhaps it is our shadow side of being, like when Darth Vader warned Luke, 'Beware the power of the dark side.'

She stands up. "Hey, you knew there was going to be my connection with him, and he would be in my life. I can't just cut him off cold down there in Honduras. That would be wrong. Let me deal with him for a little while and then we can reconnect and enjoy the day. Remember, I am here with you. I chose to be here."

My gut tells me something is off.

As I walk along the sidewalk, two young guys around twenty with lots of pimples approach me. They are decked out in white short sleeve shirts, dark blue pants and that special kind of clip-on tie usually reserved exclusively for the assistant managers of Radio Shack.

They smile and ask, "Excuse me, sir, do you have a minute?"

"Sure." I stick out my hand and introduce myself.

The first guy says, "My name is Brian." Then the second guy chuckles and says, "My name is Bryan too. But mine is spelled with a 'Y' in it."

"Are you brothers?"

More awkward chuckling, "No…"

"Are you clones?"

"What's that?" Brian asks…

"Never mind. By the way, how old are you guys?"

"Twenty." Bryan pipes in.

"Me too," says Brian.

I remove my sunglasses. "So what's up?"

"We are with the Church of Latter Day Saints and, with your permission, we would like to give you some information and if possible read something to you."

"Absolutely, but before you do can I ask you something?"

Bryan answers, "Of course."

I take a moment to breathe in the moment and my surroundings.

It is a typical Maui stellar day with a crisp blue sky. A slight salty breeze is dancing off the water and sneaking up and around us. The birds are yammering away in the large palms, trees that have borne witness to hundreds of years of human activity, from the days of lamps lit by whale oil to the obnoxiously loud fossil fuel vehicles on the road lumbering past us.

If I look closely, I can see the full moon sitting up there sleeping in the endless blue dome, catching a catnap before brilliantly coming back on duty tonight. I sweep my hand slowly and widely across this vast spectrum, like Picasso making a broad brush stroke and ask the Two B's, "What in heaven's name do you guys make of all this?"

They ponder this for a moment then Brian asks, "All of what, the town of Kihei?"

I make another vast sweep. "The mystery. The vast miracle of it all."

Bryan looks at me quite seriously and nods his head. "I guess I have never thought too much about it."

"It's really pretty amazing…" Brian chimes in.

My turn. "I feel it is so humbling, infinite, and inspiring. That its omnipresence exists far beyond any words or language we could ever attach to it. That mere words and phonetics can at best only <u>point</u> toward it. That we can't confuse the magnificence with the metaphor."

Another sweeping gesture this time specifically including the Two Bs, I point toward their nametags. Then pointing right at the name Brian I say, "This word is not you. No words could capture you."

The Two B's are nodding and earnestly hearing me out.

I continue. "Look at the moon magically sitting up there a mere 238,857 miles away…" I raise my hand slowly and point. "Now my finger is pointing at something far more transcendent then what can be known. Even the word 'moon' is just a sound that we made up. Moon, Luna…kitchen, cocina, God, Source, all pointers…"

I think I lost them but they are hanging in there.

Now I point to the tightly held literature in their pale hands and gesture toward their booklets, "May I?" Bryan hands a few to me.

I hold up the material and ask, "Is there any way to capture all of this?" Again, sweeping my hand across our moment, "In these tiny words, no matter how beautifully written, in any book?"

There is a long silence between the three of us and then Brian asks, "Can I still read you something anyway?"

I touch his shoulder and say, "Of course. But may I choose from your magic book?"

They look at each other to see if this is somehow okay, "I guess so," says a cautious Bryan.

"How about something short and sweet from The Gospel of John, say 13-34-35...

Brian takes out his Bible and thumbs through the pages, then runs his finger down to a section. "Here it is..." He looks up to me, smiles and then continues. "And Jesus said, 'A new commandment I give unto you: Love one another. As I have loved you, so you must love one another. By this everyone will know that you are my disciples, if you love one another."

I soak that in along with the ultraviolet rays that have managed to sneak through the leaves. "Pretty simple stuff. Not easy, but pretty simple."

Brian and Bryan say, "Thank you."

We then exchange a few semi-awkward hugs.

Bryan holds up the material I had handed back to him and half-heartedly asks, "You don't really need these, do you?"

"Not today. You already gave me what I need..." Then shifting gears, "Hey, how did you guys pull the Maui tour out of the missionary destination grab bag, instead of say northern Pakistan?"

They shrug their collective shoulders, "We got lucky, I guess."

"You have good karma."

"What's that?"

"You'll have to Google that one…"

They nod and Bryan writes the word down, spelling it with a 'C'.

"Hey, can I give you a quick tip for your skin?"

They seem surprised but willing, "Please…"

"Stay away from the fried foods, the fast food, the stuff with lots of chemicals in it, the cokes, and get over to the Farmer's Market once a day and eat something green."

"Will that help?"

"Absolutely… but don't hang around there trying to save any souls or the locals will probably run you off."

They eyes widen. "We have had a lot of doors slammed in our faces."

"Well, if you want to sell 'door-to-door Jesus,' you better get used to it. People probably interpret it as arrogant."

"Why?"

I take a long exhale. "Seek first to understand, then be understood."

"Is that also in the bible?" #2 asks.

I shake my head, "No, Stephen Covey a fellow Mormon once said it."

Bryan writes that down.

I put my hands on their shoulders, "So in review. Lots of mystery, green veggies, and more humility for you and me."

We shake and our little moment comes to an end.

~~~

That evening, as we get ready for bed, she once again asks, "Pauly can I sleep up there with you? I don't like it down here on the floor."

I will let you guess which part of me would love to invite her onto my mattress, but instinctively I know how dangerous that could be. It's a struggle because despite her constant pitches for cash, I am finding myself more and more drawn to her.

Yes, she is seductive and sexy, but it goes beyond that.

We have some sort of thing that is as unexplainable as the Great Mystery I was babbling about earlier to the two Mormons.

It doesn't matter to me if she is overweight or unreliable because this force remains unchanged.

Also, having her around the past couple of days has brought to light the level of my loneliness. I had grown accustomed to solo life the same way one adapts to any dull ache or great void. Our sharing meals and life dreams has awakened in me the healthy joy of cohabitation.

Yet still my inner radar caution light is on bright red.

As she strips down to her black lingerie she asks again, "Are you sure I can't sleep up there? I promise to be good." With her newly minted tan and Sophia Loren curves perfectly framed in the subtle light, it's all I can do to not break down and weep.

Long pause, then "Ah…" I quickly turn the light off. "Let's get some rest."

"Oh Pauly…"

I lay there in bed remembering how amazing she is in bed, trying to get the thought of her in that sexy underwear out of my mind.

A part of me begins to lay odds on exactly how many days remain before I cave in, have sex with her, and then sign over my life savings (The Las Vegas over and under is 5 nights).

I know that if she climbs into bed during the night like she did back in Del Mar, history will repeat itself. Since I am dealing with an apex predator, this is clearly a Custer-at-Little-Bighorn level mismatch.

A few hours later, I am awakened not by her naked form above me, but instead by an incessantly flashing light.

Her cell phone, though muted not to ring, is receiving what looks like multiple texts and calls. I close my eyes, but the flashes continue, and with each new text, my innate curiosity beckons me to peek.

Of course, I already know who it is. Adderall Man... But the voice of doubt, as active as the light on that phone since the moment she arrived, wants to know exactly what is going on.

This yearning for clarity is only augmented by the fact that so much of what she keeps telling me simply does not add up.

With my intuition sounding five alarms, I look over at her sleeping there on the floor and make a decision to take a look.

There are way too many messages to digest, so I just scroll through quickly. There are pictures sent from both of them, his of Central American villages and vistas, hers of Maui scenery and in various erotic poses. Bikini shots, underwear shots, topless shots, and phrases like, 'miss you, wish I was there, can't wait to see you again... you will love Maui."

My stomach sinks and I feel like I have been kicked.

"What the hell are you doing with my phone?" A voice rips through the darkness demanding a reckoning.

"Reading a couple of your texts. And by the way, nothing says, 'Hey, leave me alone' like a few topless shots. I can't understand why he keeps calling."

"That is none of your business. Give me that immediately."

I toss the phone on to the bed in her direction. She grabs her phone. "Did you think I would just completely cut the cord and leave him for dead?"

"You mean like you promised?" I practically hiss. "As always you have no concept of integrity or keeping your word."

It suddenly feels like the room is spinning and I must get away from this viral being, this manipulative parasite.

I turn on a light. "I told you before you came that I didn't want his energy here with us, and if you could not honor that, please do not come. I should've known better to believe you would honor any request."

She sits up. "You had no right to look at my phone and you can't control who I interact with. If you want to calmly talk about it in the morning and come to some kind of agreement, we can do that. But we are not dating anymore. I don't belong to you, and we are both free to do whatever we want."

"You are entirely correct, but I also do not have to support you for another five minutes either. You are here as my guest."

"That's your power trip and what you did to control me when we were together."

My anger seethes. "I have no idea how to consciously deal with you."

"Rather than fight all night, can we just talk about it calmly in the morning?"

"I guess so, but I doubt I can fall asleep."

She gets up and sits on the bed. "Why are you so upset? This is not about him; it's about you. It's just your ego. You are manifesting this to push me away, to blow us up. This is your doing. Just let it go, and he will go away."

I can tell she just doesn't get it. "Let me think about it and maybe I can articulate something in the morning." I take a few deep breaths.

I try to sleep but with no luck, and eventually I get up and take a long walk. The dark night illuminates a breathtaking sky filled with stars and galaxies of unimaginable size.

The scope of what I can see helps put my problems in perspective. My situation seems insignificant, but like a pebble in my shoe, creates discomfort.

I navigate around a broken fence post and on to a rugged trail leading up a hill to nowhere in particular. Walking in the cool evening air here amongst the celestial nebula helps bring me a sense of inner space.

Could I see her side? There are always two sides. What is her paradigm?

A star, light years away, shoots across the sky.

Why did I even care? A few short nights ago when she got off that plane, I felt nothing. Now it is as if she belongs to me. What is this strange sense of attachment and ownership?

Do I want her for my partner? I consider everything I know and have heard in the past few days- drinking, drugs, violence, sex clubs... and the answer is a pretty clear 'no.'

Did I hope that somehow everything that had once ailed us would be magically healed by the mystical Maui aloha and we would live happily ever after as we had once dreamed?

Yes.

At last the hopeless romantic inside of me, detached from any sense of linear reality, comes clean.

The night's stars are brilliant and bright.

I stop and take a moment to soak them in. I wonder if there is another being pondering a romantic dilemma on the other side of that sky? There must be; in fact I would think many.

Talk about universal love. How wonderful!

After a long stretch of stargazing, I turn towards home and wind my way back down the steep incline I had been climbing.

In terms of her, I still feel a lot of confusion.

Maybe it's all the mixed messages?

I want to have your children-→ Sending naked pictures to him...

Can you finance my life--→ You have no right to your boundaries or requests...

He and I are finished-→ He will always be in my life...

Addict Life = Crazy Life

My soul certainly does not have dominion over another sovereign life form.

So why am I like this with her?

I have never been this way in my other relationships.

I sort through some random feelings. I feel used, lied to, less than, and stupid. The lying and distortions draw you into the dysfunction as you try to manage it and your feelings.

Addict Life = Crazy Life

I go back to the stars.

A huge moon is now emerging above the vast specter of Haleakala. This unfolding is so spectacular that it almost makes all the night's previous craziness worthwhile…

Eventually I wander back toward home and enter as quietly as possible.

A faint voice asks, "Are you any better?"

"Yes, much better. I had a little Milky Way Therapy.'

"The candy bar?"

I smile in the darkness. "No, the galaxy. The stars are amazing here and there is a full moon filling up the night with photons. It's worth wandering outside to gaze upon in wonder. We can have a more conscious talk in the morning."

I crawl back into the bed with the curse of cold sheets. "This might be the worst part of living solo."

A small voice from the floor asks, "What, Pauly?"

"When you sleep alone and come back to bed, the sheets are frigid. I always feel a strong pang of loneliness."

"I know what you mean," she whispers.

"But you have been living with someone."

"In theory, yes. But he works nights, so I always sleep alone. Even when he is off, it is hard for him to sleep with someone, so we sleep separately."

"Really?"

"Yes..."

I take a few deep breaths. "Did you hate that situation?"

"Yes and no. Because of the Adderall he would sometimes go days without sleeping, so it was better for me to have my own room."

Thinking... God, that had to be tough.

Suddenly, I feel her arms around me, and her body pressing against me. "Pauly, I feel like I am supposed to hold you."

It takes me a moment to adjust to her proximity. I place my arms around her hands in front of me. "Thank you. I forgot how good this feels. It's been a long time since I was held."

"Really? That's sad. I have been lonely too. I expressed this to you directly whenever we spoke on the phone."

"I thought you were just trying to console me since you were with someone."

She sighs. "No, I was being honest with you. How many times did I ask you if I could come back?"

I think for a moment. "Too many times to count."

"But I kept asking even though it was harder to do each time, and it felt worse with every 'no' you spoke."

"I'm sorry, but you were always living with someone. I felt like you weren't so much moving toward me, but running from them."

"Those other people were just placeholders. There was never anyone I would actually marry or be with long term. I was waiting for you to come get me. Part of me is still waiting."

A few moments of silence hang in the air.

I put my hand over her hand. "Hey, I'm sorry I looked at your phone."

"I know you are. But there is nothing on there that I won't tell you."

"Do you still love him?"

"Yes, but not like this. I love him and care about him. I always will. He's a sweet guy and adores me. He's broken like I am. He and I sort of saved each other from our super-crazy Christian families. We found each other at rock bottom in a time that felt hopeless. He gave me a home when my family threw me out."

I exhale. "That's a lot…"

"We've known each other since we were five years old. We hung out in high school and afterward, but it was always as friends. Then we reconnected and he literally saved me from being homeless."

The breeze blows my curtains and I can smell the sea. "I'm glad he did."

"Either way, he's not for me, because we are just too different. I came here to get away from him, though I know it's going to take time to separate. We went through a lot of traumatic times, and trauma binds people strongly, even more so than happiness, so it's going to take some time to unwind this thing."

She holds me tighter and I let out a long exhale. "And he is planning on coming?"

"He wants to come, but that doesn't mean he has to. He has nowhere to go after his trip. His parents threw him out just like mine did. In a way, I feel like I owe him something. You don't need to be threatened by him."

"I can understand the draw to him. He allows you to be and do anything, and while it may upset him, he doesn't break up with you or quit on you. That has to be awfully appealing."

"That part of it is and in that way he is the opposite of you. I never felt safe with us. You loved me so much, but you had a serious flight mechanism. If I mess up, I could be exiled on an impulse. I know I do some crazy things and that I have a lot of work to do.

"True…"

Her words are soft. "But you can't create a deep loving committed relationship that way."

"No, that's why I have spent so much time in self-imposed exile." I take a very deep breath. "What a waste…"

Her words are spoken softly. "We are all so afraid of someone really seeing us, we hide our ugliness from the world."

I squeeze her hand. "Yes, but all we long for is to be seen."

"We had a lot of nights like this. I remember you being there when I felt like I didn't want to live anymore."

"I think at some point everyone has those kind of thoughts."

She sighs. "If I'm really honest, I just hate myself. My parents have always despised me and told me how terrible I am, so I've lived down to their expectations."

She lets go of me and turns the other way so I shift and hold her. She pushes my arms away, but I try again and she lets me embrace her.

I whisper into her ear, "What is so bad about you that you hate yourself?"

"Come on, you know me too well to ask me that. All of the abortions, I can't get a job and when I finally do, I get fired. Women despise me for my looks and men just want to fuck me. Alcohol, pills… God. I'm a mess and have never fit in, so I choose to check out. Remember that time my ex put a gun to my head in Spokane?"

"Yes…"

"Part of me so wished he would just pull the trigger and put an end to all this. I just screw everything up, and everyone I touch I hurt. Look at the way I am with you."

Part of me is shocked by these declarations since she has never been so forthright. I try to say something, but only silence is within me.

I hold her.

She continues. "I feel like this is who I am at my core. I am darkness, like a vampire, and there's nothing that I can do to change that."

With my face pressed against her shoulder I whisper. "I think love can heal anything, as corny as that may sound. Love can transform it-not overnight-but over time. Real love. I have to believe this to be true."

"Pauly, you are an optimist and an idealistic person, almost childlike. But I think you are wrong when it comes to me.

She softly weeps while I hold her in my arms.

As the first rays of the sun begin to drift through our window, my wounded little sparrow falls asleep in my arms.

Day Five

After such an emotional and tumultuous night, we sleep in.

Later, we wander down the street to a lovely little stretch of beach. Not much is said, a nap is taken and then a long swim.

As the water dries on our skin, her phone starts buzzing.

My words just slip out. "So when is he coming?"

"Well... nothing is set... he doesn't have to come... I promised he could come... but that doesn't mean... well, unless he insists... then I would have to honor the promise... I would have to keep my commitment..."

I sit up. "You also made me a promise."

"Well, after he left for Honduras and his family threw me out and changed the locks, I told him he didn't have to go back to those crazies, that if he had to, he could come here."

I can't help but shake my head.

"Should I call him and tell him not to come? Pauly, part of me is terrified of you leaving and me being here alone with no money or friends. I also feel a loyalty to him because he gave me a place for two years."

Something in me feels sad for her, and also disappointed. Did I want to step up and fill the void?

No.

She looks up hopefully. "What if we give him some money so he can set up his life somewhere else?"

For a moment I hold my breath. "You want me to give him money to 'not come' to Maui?"

"Well, he spent all our money in Central America, and he needs some help…"

For some strange reason I feel surprised. "He spent your money too?"

I glance around expecting a graying Rod Serling to step out from behind the nearby palm trees and start telling the audience that the two people on the beach are lost somewhere in the Twilight Zone.

As if on cue her cell phone rings. She ignores it and it rings again, and again.

"Shit. I have to take it. He's trying to figure out if there is some way for me to get these checks cashed and put them into his account. Will you cash them?"

I stand up and shake off my towel. "No, I can't do that…"

"Are you going to walk away? This will only take a couple of minutes… we need to deal with this."

"Let me get some space, I'll touch base later."

Her phone rings again. She holds up a finger as if to say, 'please wait'… but I walk away and suppress a strong desire to hold up a different finger.

The Tao of Shades

I walk slowly for a couple of miles along the coast before coming upon a weathered, friendly face sitting under a small cluster of palm trees. "Mi hermano en espíritu…"

I bow. "Master Shades."

He touches his old Red Sox cap. "Where is that beautiful girl I saw you with yesterday?"

I point down the beach. "Somewhere back there working out the details of her boyfriend's arrival in Maui."

"Sounds like a mess. Is this the girl we spoke about before?"

"Yes. She was borderline homeless so I brought her here to paradise," I gesture towards the ever-clear South Kihei blue sky, "in the hopes she could start a new life. But after a few days, I feel like a guest on the pre-iceberg Titanic."

Shades, who is wearing his usual uniform of old pants, a dark green tee shirt, and the ancient cap, laughs. "May I offer some humble counsel?"

"Of course."

He takes a long sip of water from a plastic bottle and considers the moment. "Speaking from my experience, rescues never work out. I used to say, 'If I am working harder on your life than you are, something's not right.' Are there any addiction issues?"

"Yes. How did you know?"

He waves his hand, "You live on the street you pick up a little bit of wisdom. Women that look like that don't suddenly become homeless without something sinister lurking behind the scenes. What's her deal?"

"Her last four years have been a rollercoaster of pills and alcohol."

He winces. "Has she ever sought any treatment or gone to meetings?"

"Not to date." I think for a moment then add, "That's just the part I know."

He ponders my words. "You'll go crazy trying to stay sane with an addict in your life."

Thinking for a minute. "I definitely gravitate towards women in constant distress who happen to look like Playboy bunnies."

He smiles and nods in agreement. "That used to be my type, but I had to quit. It was an expensive habit, especially emotionally." A couple of teenagers walk by us blaring insanely loud rap music. BOOM-BOOM-BOOM! Old Shades shakes his head slowly. "Assholes."

I continue. "If I'm honest, these high-octane addict types are always more compelling than the so-called 'normal' women I run across. Does this make me insane?"

Shades holds up his hand. "Maybe not... a touch of crazy exists in all of us."

I shake my head. "For some reason I have found it challenging to manifest what would appear to be a normal relationship."

"Normal? As in?"

"Well, here is what I imagine: Two people meet and seem to hit it off. There are no huge sparks, but a general interest in a healthy sort of way. Things are kind of casual at first then become almost imperceptibly more and more serious.

"In the meantime, they both act like adults and display healthy boundaries, while finding time for friends, the gym, and other pursuits. They do 'normal' things like; go to dinner with other couples or participate in walk-a-thons for incurable diseases.

"According to my extensive research, after about two years, there is a logical discussion where they move forward on a deeper level. Not long afterward, a ridiculously overpriced stone on a high interest payment plan is procured and they get 'engaged.' At that point the bride's mother, for years frustrated by her husband's long list of shortcomings, moves into a semi-manic state which culminates in a bad wedding band playing too loudly, while several inebriated overweight people dance badly.

So I have to wonder, 'why can't this happen to me?"

"That is fucking hysterical! Stop it, you are killing me." He is gasping and patting his thigh. "No mas…"

"Wait. Here is what usually happens: I meet some insanely attractive woman who radiates erotic charisma. She is either one step ahead of the authorities, between lovers (I'm talking minutes here), needs a place to live, is way too much fun, both in and out of the bedroom, but then it eventually burns out.

"I call it The Lightning Strikes Dating Formula. It's a load of fun, but sadly in the end leaves you feeling like you've been struck by lightning. (Not fun).

"Honestly, I have never had one before like this gal, but I am sure one is more than enough."

Old Shades takes a long breath. "And you brought her here with hope…"

"I did indeed… but obviously I was just enabling an addict who…"

The sage cuts me off. "No. It's a thin line between being empowering and enabling. I can tell your heart is in the right place. Ever help anyone, guy or gal, whose life took off afterwards?"

I think for a moment. "Yes, of course, lots of people…"

"There you go. By the way, the only way you found out the truth about this was through trying. Otherwise, you would have never known, and trust me on this, a lifetime of regret would have haunted you more than a few crazy days in paradise.

"Besides, I told you to lean into love, and you did. Now it is alright to lean back and let chaos move on."

I take a few moments to digest the enormous wisdom in my friend's words. "You're right."

He looks off toward the water for a few moments. "Of course, you just have to be a little more discerning, but it's hard when you love someone and there is history, not to mention that kind of beauty. Remember all you ever are doing is learning."

"I am…"

"It's important to know when to put a few more chips on the center of the table, and when to fold up a bad hand and walk out of the casino without looking back."

"The Tao of Shades."

He takes off his cap and makes a grand gesture. "Given for the price of our next cup of coffee."

The Cautionary Tale

Returning to the house there is no sign of the Broken Girl. I sit down at my desk and take out my journal. A moment later there is a soft tap on my door.

A silver haired man of about sixty, who rents the room down the hall, enters. "Hello, my friend. Do you have a minute?"

"Of course."

"By the way, thank you for the excellent tip on that secret beach out past Wailea. The snorkeling was fantastic."

I put down my pen. "Did you see many turtles?"

He nods. "Too many to count, and more colorful fish than the mind could imagine. Hey, you seem like a good guy. Do you mind if I share a couple of things?"

"Please."

He pulls up my extra chair, sits down, and takes a deep breath. "I've been observing some things around the house this week between you and the visiting girl."

"I hope we haven't disturbed you or the others."

"Not at all. But I have had a few conversations with your guest. She shared some things and I subtly inquired about her various lifestyle choices."

I nod. "Yes, I remember you two had a really long talk a couple of afternoons ago, and then again yesterday morning."

"Yes. But before I express a few things, first let me share a slice of my own history."

He looks up at the ceiling as if she searching his database for a place to begin.

He lets out a slow breath. "About thirty years ago, I started dating this absolutely beautiful woman. At the time, I was working as a psychologist for the state of Connecticut and she was a nurse. Well, we didn't date for long because I discovered she was mentally unbalanced. But a few months later on my birthday, she called and invited me over to her home for dinner."

I lean back in my chair. "Uh-oh..."

"You already see it coming? She cooked me a fabulous dinner, we drank too much wine, things got out of hand, fireworks exploded and then I went my short-lived merry way."

He shakes his head, takes his glasses off, and rubs his temples. "I got a call three months later saying she was pregnant and going to have our baby."

"Did you get married?"

"No, thank God. We tried living together for a couple of months, but I'm telling you she is out of her mind. But because of that one evening, I have had to deal with her from crisis to crisis and back again, on a weekly basis for years. Years! She has made my life a mess."

He looks across the room at the mirror on the wall. "It's probably aged me by at least a decade. The whole saga has been a nightmare I wouldn't wish on anybody."

I feel a chill go down my spine and realize that, despite of all this temporary unpleasantness, up to this point I have been let off the cosmic hook with a light slap on the wrist.

I glance at The Cautionary Tale sitting across the table, a mere shell of a man, with his white hair and weary eyes, and an overwhelming feeling of compassion rises within me.

He continues. "May I make a few professional observations?"

I gesture with my hand. "Please..."

"Your gal appears to be on some kind of, or perhaps several, medications with counteracting symptoms. I also hear her outside my window late into the evening plotting with some guy about coming here and starting a new life together. Do you know about that?"

Some of the air goes out of me. "I literally just found out."

"Be careful because I believe she is a borderline personality. They are cunning and very dangerous. You might want to hide any credit cards or checkbooks and I'll warn the other people in the house."

"Are you sure?"

"I can spot them a mile away, both from my work and sadly from personal experience. The 'borderline' embodies the worst combination of a sociopath and a narcissist. There's no helping them because they assume no responsibility and leave a wide trail of destruction."

"Oh heavens…"

"They usually have multiple addictions. Does she?"

"Yes…"

"Struggle with eating disorders?"

"She does…"

"Sometimes will cut herself?"

"Yes, unfortunately…"

"Will steal without conscience?"

"Yes, even from her family…"

"Manipulate, especially with sex?"

"Well thank God there is an upside…"

He chuckles for a moment. "I guess it's good to find some humor in the tragedy."

"You sound clairvoyant."

"No, it's just classic textbook symptoms. Remember, this is what I do for a living. You need to be careful and get her out of here as soon as possible."

I check my drawer to see if my wallet is still there. It is. "Thank you, brother."

He leans in. "She is exceptionally beautiful and will probably use whatever means possible to get what she wants."

"That's been her pattern." Part of me is in shock, another part is grateful, another wants to weep, and another to immediately change the locks.

He gets up. "So my friend, learn from my mistake and don't throw your life away on someone like this for a few moments of fleeting pleasure." He holds up his hands. "One night of fun could equal thirty-plus years of pain."

"So the girl with the angel face is a sociopath. Are you sure there is no hope for her?"

He shakes his head. "Technically yes, but probably not. If she has not gotten help by now, she probably never will. Also, being so lovely makes it hard for her to hit bottom."

I look around the room then back at him. "And she doesn't even think she has a problem."

"That is a classic part of the borderline personality. They always view themselves as the victim."

For a moment I search my soul. "Is there *anything* I can do to help this person? I mean this is a human being I deeply care about. Someone I once built a life with."

"I'm sorry. Not if she doesn't feel that she needs help. But again, at least you don't have to be tied to her for the rest of your days. Hell, my mistake still calls once a month trying to get me to pay for something, loan her some money, or just to rant. You escaped the net for now, so don't swim back into it."

I stand up and give The Cautionary Tale a hug. "Thank you. This is a huge help. I guess the universe moved an in-house expert into my home for 24-hour emotional tech support."

He opens his arms. "I'm here if you need me, with 35 years of tragic experience. By the way, I read your book and it was terrific."

The upbeat change of topic catches me a bit off guard. "Thank you."

"You're welcome. So I have to ask, whatever happened to The Miracle?"

"Well, currently she spends her evenings outside your window talking to a guy in Central America about coming to Maui."

He looks completely aghast. "No way. That's not her, and don't even joke about that."

I give him a long, sad look. "Brother, I so wish I was."

The Cautionary Tale is clearly rattled. "Oh man, I had no idea this girl was The Miracle. I am heartbroken for you. She's really The Miracle?"

I put my hand on his shoulder. "My friend, she once was, but I believe she has now become The Mirage."

At a loss for words, he shakes his head.

The two of us make our way out of my space to the living room.

The Cosmic Hoarder comes in holding a box of some odd looking junk. "Hey there, have you guys seen my hand-powered popcorn maker around?"

I shake my head. "Remember, I never use the kitchen. But if I see it, I'll let you know."

"Thanks." She looks in a couple of cabinets, then asks, "How long is that girl going to stay here with you?"

"Not much longer. How come?"

"I don't get a good vibe from her, like she is on drugs or something. I don't trust her."

This is beginning to feel like Life is doing an intervention. "I'll get her out as soon as possible."

I go back into my room and gather up my checkbooks and hide them in a closet on the far side of the house. A part of my heart breaks when I consider this was a person I once shared a dream with and considered a potential life partner.

God, what happened to my girl?

That night I go solo to an Aloha Potluck at an opulent home overlooking the coast. Everything about the evening is magical, but I find myself distracted and without much of an appetite.

The party hosts, a middle-aged couple who are friends of friends, introduce me to their son and his girlfriend. The young couple quickly recognizes me as the author of one of their favorite books. "Oh my god! I can't believe you're at my parent's party. Mom, Dad, this is the guy who wrote that book we are always talking about, *Hitchhiking With Larry David*. How did you end up here in Maui?"

I manage a smile. "I was in Los Angeles and felt the pull of the island."

The young girl lights up and scans the guests on the expansive lawn and around the pool. "So which one of those lovely ladies is The Miracle? I so fell in love with the two of you and it lifted my heart when you reunited at the end of the book. Thank goodness you guys came to your senses." She playfully pokes me, "Especially you! Wow, what a love story."

The young guy jumps in. "We quote from your book and have shared it with a lot of people. There should be a copy here. Maybe you could sign it for us?"

"Of course…"

The young girl asks, "Did you guys get married? That must be book two. You are writing a sequel I hope." More looking at the crowd, "Come on, point her out to me…"

What do I say? Should I pop this beautiful bubble they have so sweetly constructed around me, and all of us? If I only had a dollar for everyone who either wrote me with some version of this interaction, or how many people were rooting for us, and how deeply they cared.

Heavens, what have I done and do I dare share such a sad and sorrowful outcome?

More importantly, what about the girl I used to love so deeply, and still care about with every fiber of my being?

Yes, I brought her here, but now what? Did I really think that a simple plane ride over the ocean and a few days in my presence would undo a lifetime of pain and the deep scars that haunt this poor soul?

Now what?

I feel empty and powerless.

One of the people in my circle says, "It looks like we lost you."

I recover. "I was thinking about The Miracle. Yes, she is on the island, but she is back at our place. She's been going through some changes and wasn't up to coming tonight. I promise to pass on your generous words to her the moment I walk through the door."

The young couple slaps a high five. "I knew they made it!"

I feel the bottom drop out of me.

One of the other people asks, "Is there a sequel?"

"Not yet. I've been reluctant to follow the first one with anything other than a coloring book."

Cue the laughter. "Seriously," the young man says, "What about writing another piece?"

First, I point towards my head. "Right now, it's only up here. Oh, wait. " I then point towards my heart. "Actually it's in here."

Cue the sighs.

After the party I am tempted to keep driving down the hill and straight into the ocean. I know life is messy, but between the mythology around the book and the reality of what is waiting for me at home, I feel at a complete loss to bridge such an enormous gap.

Back at the house I enter our room to find her on Skype with him. The moment is awkward as she tries to get him off the computer as quickly as possible without acknowledging that I am present.

She has to say 'let me call you back' about a half dozen times before simply closing the laptop down. A moment later, her phone lights up.

Her words to me are a rapid-fire blur of non-related subjects mixed with other disjointed topics. Once the verbal dust somewhat settles, it's time for me to do what must be done and pull the plug on this tragic experiment.

With her sitting across from me on the bed, and my back literally against the wall I say, "I'm sorry but this is not what we agreed upon. So I must ask you to leave."

Her eyes widen. "Now?"

I shake my head. "No, not this evening. But you can't stay here. The people in the house are not comfortable with you here, and neither am I. I can buy you a ticket back to Seattle, and you can depart tomorrow."

"But I have nowhere to stay there. My parents changed their locks when I left... I don't..."

"I'm sorry. Do you have any money?"

"A few dollars. Will you cash those Adderall checks for me?"

Again I shake my head. "I'm not going to do anything illegal. What about your share of the money that was in your joint account? Is all of it really gone?"

She looks shaken. "He spent that on gifts for me."

"So he is definitely coming here?"

"He doesn't have to. We could even avoid him when he does. He doesn't even know where we are on Maui. There is no way he could…"

I cut her off. "I'm not going to live like Bonnie and Clyde. When is he supposed to get here?"

"I have no idea."

I know she is lying. "Tell me the truth, or I will kick you out tonight."

She pauses. "In ten days."

"Was he always coming?"

"Well, I don't… he never…"

"Please, just the truth if you want another night or day here…"

She bows her head. "Yes, he was always coming."

For a few minutes, I let this sink in. She goes back to babbling, but I completely tune her out. In the meantime, I wonder what to do with her. She won't leave if he is coming, but she can't stay here.

Finally I come back from my inner contemplation. "Well, let's sleep on it tonight. We will come up with a plan in the morning. Starting tomorrow I want you to figure out where you will move to as soon as possible."

She touches my arm. "It doesn't have to be like this."

"Sadly, I'm afraid it does."

She picks up her phone and leaves the room. I turn out the light, and to my surprise fall sound asleep in a matter of minutes.

Day Six

Fixing A Hole Where The Pain Gets In

Through some strange blessing/curse I have never been able to drink or take mind-altering drugs. It's just not in my makeup. This does not make me any better than the next bloke. This gift/malady has allowed me to stay very clear, which is a wonderful/terrible thing because I get to feel all life's joy/sorrow so acutely.

But everyone has something to distract them from The Hole.

A brief history of my Distraction Laundry List:

1) Academic excellence.
2) Sports stardom.
3) Chasing gorgeous women.
4) Playing music professionally.
5) Sex.
6) Money.
7) Spending money chasing gorgeous women for sex.
8) Spiritual growth.
9) Fixing gorgeous/broken women for sex in the name of spiritual growth.
10) Writing.
11) Making money writing about my experience, trying to fix gorgeous/broken women, in exchange for sex, in the name of spiritual growth.

So sharing time with The Mirage allows me to hit a lot of my hot buttons.

When I exert enormous amounts of time and energy trying to save/fix/educate/help/ and enable her, there is a whole lot less awareness of my own Inner Hole.

As obvious as this is to me now, I realize I have been sublimely sailing down the River of Denial.

She can never be 'fixed.' So, it is the perfect hopeless cause.

But here I am talking about her again. See? I avoided The Hole within me by focusing on the closest available addict/sociopath.

The great spiritual teacher Eckhart Tolle, (*The Power of Now & The New Earth*) calls this Hole, 'The Pain Body.' As they say, 'a thorn by any other name, is still a thorn.'

When mine is alive and prowling around for fresh meat, it prefers to focus on someone else, but in a pinch, it is more than happy to maul me.

I leave the sleeping Mirage and go for a long walk on Big Beach.

I decide to have a talk with The Hole.

Me: "Hello, Hole."

Hole: "Hello. May I first say, you are such a worthless piece of shit. What have you ever accomplished?"

Me: "I could vainly list all my achievements hoping you might call off the dogs…"

Hole: "But I would say, that's pathetic. Because, if you weren't so lazy/stupid/cursed/fucked up, you would be worth billions of dollars by now and would have finally brought some peace to the Middle East."

Me: "There you go…"

Hole: "And look at you drifting all over the place without a home of your own."

Me: "Wait, I owned a home and you said I was a loser for buying into all the propaganda like everyone else."

Hole: "That's beside the point. By now you should have bought several homes. Speaking of which, how come you're not married and have never had any children? What kind of loser are you that no one would want to be with you? When are you going to grow up?"

Me: "You have me on that one. But everyone I have ever cared about, you turned on for not being perfect or good enough for you, not me. Your insatiable wanting/craving/longing/lusting has left me isolated and lonely."

Hole: "I can't help it if everyone is so broken/messed up/stupid/unconscious. Don't you see? I have been trying to protect you. I built these thick, high walls to keep you safe?"

Me: "But what's the difference between a fortress and a prison if the person or inmate cannot control when we can get in or out?"

Hole: "You have me on that one."

Me: "It's lonely in here. Yes, it's peaceful, quiet, calm, easy, and the view is quite beautiful here in Maui, but I think I have had enough solitary confinement for one lifetime. I want to dive in, to fail miserably, to be held in my darkest hour, and more importantly, hold someone else when they fall apart. I'm tired of hiding. I can no longer run anymore."

Hole: "Are you insane?"

Me: "If it means saying 'Yes' to pain/glory/suffering/ecstasy/bliss/death, then call me what you will. I surrender to Life, even if it means being crushed. Besides, I would rather die gloriously in battle pursuing a noble cause like love, then to wither away moment by moment in this asylum by myself playing it safe."

Hole: "Why don't you get a dog?"

Me: "I'm thinking of putting out a healthy dose of unconditional love. Selfless acts that do not directly benefit me, being completely open and vulnerable…

Hole: "Uh-oh…"

Me: "Being in a committed relationship with a fellow Brokenite…"

Hole: "Brokenite? Did you just make that up?"

Me: "Yes…"

Hole: "Technically I can't compliment you, but if I could…"

Me: "I used to think being solo, alone, completely self-sufficient, was a sign of great strength, but now I think maybe the opposite is true. Yes, you have to have your own act together, but what good is a story?-and really we are just manifested life stories-what good is a story, if it can't be shared?"

Hole: "Ahhh… well…"

Me: "Really. What good is a story if it can't be shared?"

Hole: "Why don't you do what everyone else does? Take some kind of pill or buy something, anything to fill me up. That's why I love advertising because it convinces people that they can fill me externally. And all those silly magazines that make people believe being rich/beautiful/famous will fill me completely. I think Elvis, God rest his soul, proved that one to be a lie."

Me: "I have decided to live and be openly broken. I need to find a girl from my tribe to take a trip with."

Hole: "Thailand?"

Me: "No, intimacy."

I leave The Hole on the beach and return to the house to grab my snorkeling gear.

She is in my room taking a few pictures of her sister's stolen computer so I ask, "Are you really going to sell that heisted laptop?"

The Mirage shakes her head. "I have no choice if you kick me out. How else can I afford to live here?"

"How much are you asking for it?"

"I'll take $1000. It's loaded with software programs and probably cost close to $4000 new. Do you want to buy it?"

I shake my head. "No, I'm not going to purchase stolen goods from you. Honestly, you have to give it back. Think about your sister, flesh and blood, and your grandfather, who you proclaim as your patron saint. Don't go that low, just send it back with a nice apology. I'll even pay for the shipping."

She puts the computer back in its box and then takes off her warm up top to reveal her miniscule black bikini top and ample tan cleavage bursting forth.

OK, here comes some kind of $$$ pitch.

She then lets down her hair and shakes it out.

This must be a BIG ask.

"Pauly, can we talk calmly for a minute?"

Calmly?

My life continues to take on a surreal quality. "Please, go ahead."

"I know you were planning to leave for L.A. soon. Is there a way you would let the two of us move into this room? And if you want my opinion, you need to get there as soon as possible. Major things will start happening for your career once you commit to being in Hollywood full-time."

I sit down and decide to play along this time yet with a more light-hearted approach. "Maybe I could leave in a couple of days, though I paid for the remaining three weeks. That would give you guys a head start."

She perks up and then sits down next to me. "Would you consider paying just one more month's rent for me? That would give us a roof and seven weeks to get on our feet."

I frown, "But it makes me sad to think of the two of you right here in my bed fucking your brains out while I work hard to pay the rent."

She is suddenly serious. "Oh, if you say so, he would never stay here. I can promise you that."

"I guess if you gave me your word."

How can she not tell I am completely joking around?

"Pauly, do you know what I really want?"

I shake my head because honestly at this point I have no idea what she will say next... for us to get married, join the circus, go to a sex club, start a chain letter...

"I want you to buy me that simple Tiffany's ring as a symbol of our love."

Wow, that was out of left field...

"Oh sweetheart, what a touching thought! Our love is simple like that little ring. How much was that again?"

Now excited, "Less than $400!"

"Is that all? That's nothing for such an important symbol." I pick up an official-looking piece of paper sitting on the bed with her name on it. "What's this?"

She takes it from me. "I applied for food stamps today."

"Already?"

"How am I going to eat?"

I take on a deeply concerned look. "Gosh, I hadn't thought of that. You know, I should probably leave you with, I don't know, about $1000 cash just for operating expenses. But you would have to promise you wouldn't give any money to Adderall Man. It would only be for you."

She looks very serious. "Of course. I promise."

"Give me your word?" I stick out my hand.

Nodding, and then shaking my hand, "Absolutely."

"So let me see here: Take over my room immediately, a month's rent, the ring, spending money, I think that covers everything. Is there anything else?"

"What about your scooter?"

"Good thinking. You will need some way to get around."

"Yes, and I could pay you for it later." She leans towards me. "Pauly, will you do it for us?"

I stand up. "I am going to grab this gear and go for a long swim. Then when I see my Spirit Guide, Shelly The Sea Turtle, I will ask her what she thinks of all of this."

Her face turns completely sour. "That is so mean. I can't believe how selfish you are."

"And let me guess. You would do it for me, right?"

"You know I would…"

"True."

"Will you at least cash these Adderall checks?"

"Let me ask Shelly about that one too."

Exit stage right.

I grab my snorkeling gear and head down to the ocean. Maybe the salt water can wash me clean of this toxic situation.

The ocean's surface resembles an aqua sheet of glass embodying the opposite end of the spectrum to my inner turbulence. After adjusting my gear, I take the plunge and enter a different world.

Unfortunately, The Hole has decided to come along for a swim and kick my sorry ass: "How the hell could you bring that lying piece of shit to paradise? Everything was going so well and you had to mess it up. You realize you have not done one bit of healing? You are right back at square one. How could you think she would be any different? She's even worse. What a sociopath. Boy, you sure know how to pick them."

First her, and now The Hole! Rather than engage in a protracted debate, I decide the best course of action is to swim out and find a very hungry tiger shark. I rationalize this choice as a form of natural selection. After all, Universal Life would not want someone as stupid as me breeding and reproducing more idiots.

The Hole considers this scenario and reluctantly agrees.

As I swim towards my imminent demise, my focus shifts to the magical surroundings in front of me. The temperature of the water is perfect. Visibility excellent. My body feels strong and alive.

After a while, The Hole backs off, shrinks and then vanishes.

My breathing becomes deep and rhythmic, rising and falling like the very slight swell that gently lifts me. The light of our closest star strikes the water's surface and fragments into the most fascinating patterns, all of them dancing on the sand beneath me. This phenomenon creates a never-ending series of geometric patterns, prisms, structures, and shapes.

All utterly unique to the moment and constantly changing... just like me... just like everything.

I realize the light passing through the water has simply been slowed down, and so have I.

The Hole makes a momentary comeback. "Hey, maybe you should watch out for sharks. Oh, and you still should not have brought that woman here..."

Duly noted...

A few minutes later, I come upon a vast civilization constructed of coral and creatures that appear much too busy to take notice of me or my menial cares. A multi-colored eel tries to dislodge an urchin from his fortifications, as fish of all sizes and hues move through the cracks and crevices of the kingdom.

All of us warmly held and nourished by the Mother.

The water supports me as I float along weightless in mind and body.

I feel light and free.

On some level, I wonder if drifting here so effortlessly triggers in me the memory of my own mother's womb and those carefree days as a water creature living in embryonic bliss?

I go within and look for the Hole. It's gone like the bubbles from my snorkel heading towards the surface.

A silent, inner laugh arises spontaneously within me.

I am such an idiot: For thinking any of my tiny little shit matters, for taking it all too seriously, for bringing her here and then taking her choices personally, for reacting from my pain, and for thinking I could not be human. I made a choice and tried to do something I thought was right for someone I care about. It happened the way it happened, and now I am right here.

The last part is crucial; I mean, if you had to have heartbreak and disappointment, it's always best to do it in a tropical location with some of the best beaches in the world.

Hey, at least I got that part right.

Out of the corner of my left eye, I suddenly catch a very large shape within a foot of me and instinctively jump in primal defense. Shark? No, a giant sea turtle has floated up to check me out.

My attention turns to my floating mascot who is quite large.

In weightless wonder I study her form, closely observing the patterns on her shell and those prehistoric eyes. She looks ancient and in many ways, she is. I float within two feet of her as both of us are intensely still.

A few moments later, she tilts her head up and takes a long breath.

Oxygen, a common thread between us. I smile silently and without movement.

In her vast life, what has she seen? What did she know? Why was she here?

Why was I here?

A large school of fish on their way to somewhere else slowly passes around and under us. If she took any notice of them, she was subtle about it.

Like anything, the more I gaze at her, the more beautiful she becomes. What a gorgeous life form.

For some reason I am momentarily transported back to my time in Manhattan and the confines of big city life; the noise, energy, crowds, confusion, cabs, horns, and chaos. I realize in hindsight how contracted my Being felt there, in relation to the vast expansion I am breathing in here.

A deep wave of gratitude washes over and through me.

All the stuff back there in Kihei with The Mirage seems small and nonsensical, easily dealt with from a place of compassion and healthy boundaries. No hate is required. My mind nods and I return my Presence to my underwater sanctuary. I notice my breathing has become long, slow and deep.

My Turtle Guide is still here. A study in motionless grace...

The creature with the hard shell takes another long breath and descends a few feet in front of me, swimming slowly along the coral.

I decide to invite myself along behind her. The water is only about ten feet deep so I am not that far above her. She glides silently and effortlessly through the H^2O, utilizing millions of years of trial and error, and genetic upgrades.

She is perfectly designed for this.

With her in the lead, we move through canyons of coral, all alive and colorful, while being surrounded by fish of every Crayola color one can imagine. Bright and brilliant, these luminous beings are everywhere.

I wonder what force or entity could imagine and create such beauty, certainly not a small and petty mind.

No one in the aquatic kingdom seems to mind me passing through town as a conscientious observer.

A random floating thought/observation: I think there are three aspects to the dynamic between the Mirage and myself:

1. Who I believe she is and project upon her.
2. Who she seems to be in relation to me.
3. Who she really is separate from one and two.

Projection	Reality
Spiritually based	Worldly
Non-materialistic	Desires expensive things
Striving to be healthy	Active in addiction
Tells the truth	Compulsive Liar
Trustworthy	Dishonest
Loyal	Detached

In some strange coincidence, all of my projections align perfectly with my own values and morality.

An inner key turns and there comes a lovely insight: So one night in Del Mar I decided to cast a stunning young woman as my love interest in the Pauly Life Dream. When in reality her inner values were always radically different from mine.

She could look the part, but never live it.

What a terrible burden for me to place upon another being.

I also realize her survival skill is to morph into what her Host Organism needs her to become. She is a highly adept and extremely effective romantic/relationship chameleon. When she is with me, The Mirage becomes the 'spiritual seeker' on a quest towards higher learning. When connected to the alcoholic drug pusher, she becomes an addict living on the edge. When she was married, she became the dutiful Christian wife.

There is no true north, no stable center, no core value or character to live from so she bounces around the spectrum between polarities like a free radical.

She lives in a perpetual state of survival, lunging from crisis to crisis, one step ahead of homelessness and at the mercy of random men like myself who come and go. She doesn't have the strength to do it on her own, or so she believes, so she always ends up taking short cuts.

Only to discover they always lead to the same dead end.

It is impossible for me to hate her. How could I?

However, I wouldn't be writing them a survival check. Shuck and Jive would have to figure it out without my largess. The real tragedy is that beneath all the damage, there is a beautiful soul crying out for love.

Just like all of us...

Yes, that may also be my projection. But there were too many moments where the level of transparency and authenticity transcended the limitations of the superficial human persona.

Back in the warm water moment, my Sea Turtle Guide ascends next to me and makes eye contact. Two creatures from the same womb of Being, sharing a few breaths together along the cosmic life path, just like The Mirage and myself.

To project judgment on either one of them feels like a karmic violation.

The old lady takes another long breath and descends to the ocean's floor. From there she finds a cave to rest in. She will be safe there. I hover above her for a while, unwilling to let go and bring this silent voyage to an end.

But all things must pass, and so, with a reluctant heart, I dive down to bid her fond farewell. I find her motionless there in the crevice. We share just one more moment together… and then I surface.

Sadly, it's time to go back.

Sam I Am

An hour later, I am sitting on my beach towel watching the sun play hide and seek with a lovely array of clouds while a large group of whales swims slowly by in the distance.

A black lab sneaks up behind me and drops a wet, sand-covered tennis ball in my lap. He then shakes his wet fur all over me. A voice calls in the near distance, "Oh my God, I am so sorry! Juno, come here, boy."

A tan, fit man with dark skin comes over and captures the friendly beast. "I'm sorry. He is just a puppy and in the process of flunking out of obedience school." He sticks out his hand, "Hello, my name is Sam."

"No worries. I love dogs and especially characters like this." I give him a squeeze and then fire his tennis ball into the sea. Juno turns and makes a mad dash for the water. SPLASH!

"Are you visiting?" Sam asks.

"In a sense. I'm here for about three months then have to return to Los Angeles. How about you?

"I've lived here for about ten years. I teach yoga and meditation around the island."

"Two essentials for happiness and well-being."

He makes a funny face. "I wish more people felt that way. How is Maui treating you?"

"For the most part well. It was kind of tough at first energetically. Then there was a lot of flow, followed by a little bit of self-inflicted suffering."

Sam raises an eyebrow. "Maui, she will bring up your stuff."

"Maui is kind compared to my ex-girlfriend."

"Does she live here?"

"She's here now and wants to stay. She was feeling suicidal in Seattle, so I brought her out here."

"Suicidal in Seattle-wasn't that a Tom Hanks, Meg Ryan film?" Sam winks.

I nod. "Sounds like something Hollywood would release as a sequel."

Sam looks down and thinks for a moment. "So she was suicidal in Seattle and you brought her out to lighten things up?"

I burst out laughing. "Exactly. She's only been here a couple of days and is already causing massive chaos and dissonance. What a shock. I am trying to figure out a way to jettison her as soon as possible."

"Rescuing never works, take it from someone who learned the hard way. You know, there is a cheap youth hostel you can park her in if you need the space."

Juno returns with the ball, puts it down, and then as required by canine law, shakes off all his water right next to me. Undeterred I pick it up and throw it out again towards the setting sun. "Thanks for the tip on the hostel. Do they have a psychiatric ward?"

He raises an eyebrow. "That bad?"

"Worse. She's gone off the deep end on me. Funny, she was never anything close to this bad when we were together. In fact, we had a wonderful couple of years way back when. I feel stupid for self-contaminating this tropical paradise with her addiction-based bullshit."

"Don't be too hard on yourself. The human heart is strange creature. And hey, sometimes when we give things a chance, they surprise us and work. At least you won't ever wonder what might have been."

I put my hand on his shoulder, "You are very kind to say that and you're right about erasing any doubt. Thank you."

Sam shakes his head. "You are most welcome. Maui is a magnet for addicts and deadbeats. They are everywhere."

"I have met several people with these huge, grandiose plans to save the world, yet they don't have a single dollar in their pocket. It almost feels like some people get caught in the bottom of the drain so to speak. You know the stuff left there after you wash the dishes?"

"That's a good analogy. I call them Maui Driftwood. The best we can do is be kind and compassionate in our view on all things. We can't judge."

"No Sam, we can't. If I'm honest, a bad break here or there and things might have been radically different for me."

"You and all of us, but for the grace of God."

Juno is back and this time, in an effort to spread the love around, shakes off on Sam.

"Bad dog! Bad boy!" He scolds him while smiling. Juno's tail never stops wagging. "I better get this juvenile delinquent back to his crate." Sam reaches into his pocket. "Here's my card. Send me a text with your number and we can grab lunch sometime, or maybe you can come to one of the meditations I lead."

"I would love to."

"Huli pau! Which is Hawaiian for 'cheers' or 'good to meet you.' It was a pleasure."

"Mahalo, my friend."

Sam splits and the sun slips slowly beneath the surface.

Day Seven

My phone rings with a number I don't recognize. "Hello."

"Is this Paul?"

"Yes."

"Paul, this is Jim Bohannon."

I pause and let this information sink in. Silence.

The voice on the phone speaks. "Hello, are you there?"

"Mr. Bohannon. What an honor."

"Heavens, please call me Jim."

"Jim, I used to stay up all night with your 'Open Phone America' radio show. I can't believe I am speaking with you."

"You are too kind. Well, I just finished reading the most amazing book titled, *Hitchhiking With Larry David*, and would love to have you come on my nationally-syndicated talk show.

"We broadcast on hundreds of stations and the Armed Forces Network all over the world. This would be an excellent opportunity to share your story with my audience."

Silence… and then, "I'm in shock. Thank you. I would love to be on your program. Oh wait, I just remembered the book is being re-released in hardcover by Gotham/Penguin in a couple of months. Is there any chance we can do the interview then?"

"So you got a major publishing deal?"

"I did."

"Congratulations. Of course we can do the program then, I can even time the release for the very day it comes out."

"Mr. Bohannon…"

"Please call me Jim."

"Yes, Jim. You are extremely kind and generous."

"Paul, it will be fun."

"May I ask you how you discovered my work?"

He pauses. "It is actually a wonderful little story. A summer ago you were on a beach in Martha's Vineyard and you started chatting with a dear friend of mine named Gary Nunn. In an act of kindness you gave him one of your first copies.

Well, he and I go back over forty years and worked together at a small radio station in Missouri. Through a lot of miles and even more time, Gary and I have remained close. Gary read it, raved about it, and then passed it on to me.

I have to tell you, it's a great piece of writing. You made me laugh out loud, but you also brought tears to my eyes. There is also a lot of wonderful, feel-good philosophy woven throughout it that I believe will lift people up."

"Jim, you just made my month."

"I will send you a note and contact your publisher. May I ask if there is a second book in the works?"

"I believe there is. In fact, I might be in the middle of living out a large part of it this week."

He chuckles on the end of the line. "So is that a good or bad thing?"

"Right now the jury is still out, so I'll have to let you know when I see you."

"Well I look forward to hearing all about it. Have yourself a wonderful day."

We hang up and I literally pinch myself. Isn't life just filled with crazy magic? As if on cue, a gigantic whale shoots from the sea and crashes back into the water.

"Amen." I say out loud.

I take a long, lovely drive on my scooter along the water toward Big Beach. Once again the weather is Chamber of Commerce perfect.

I come upon a small stand with a canopy over it and a makeshift sign saying, 'Fresh Cut Pineapple.'

Why not?

Pulling over the proprietor greets me warmly. "Aloha, my friend. Care for some of Maui's finest?"

"Yes sir, my brother."

He pauses. "You look familiar. Where do I know you from? Are you "Kama'aina?"

I nod. "Yes, I live here. In fact you taught me the meaning of that word, literally and figuratively."

He cocks his head then smiles. "Mr. Crazy but not bad crazy." He hugs me. "Pehea 'oe?"

"Means...?"

"How are you?"

I look up at the sun. "Haleakala has also captured my spirit."

"Just like she did the sun. How beautiful." He hands me some pineapple. "Try some of this."

The local fruit is sweet and melts in my mouth. "Oh my! This is good."

"Good for your soul too. So you hung around." He points at my scooter. "And I see you got yourself a nice little ride, too. Don't let the daydreaming Haoles run into you."

We both grin.

I take another bite of heaven. "Kai, did you quit driving the cab?"

"No, no. I do several things to keep me out of trouble and put bread on the table. Maui can be a tough place to make it."

"In more ways than one. Sometimes I feel like her energy just kicks my ass."

He nods, "She will do that. Maui brings our long buried ghosts up to hopefully heal."

"Or you can make it easy and just fly the ghost here…"

"Sounds like girl trouble…"

"Oh yes, I'm in the middle of a mess at the moment."

"The girl from the book?"

I'm a little shocked. "How did you know?"

"After we met I bought it online. It's a nice little piece of writing, my friend. Made me think about a lot of things. So you brought your Miracle to Maui?"

"I did…"

"And…?"

"Same shit, different day… check that, even worse!"

He shakes his head. "We've all been there brother, 'O ia mau no. Or as you might say, 'same as usual.' These ladies are a crazy species but we can't seem to live without them." He hands me some more pineapple and I indulge. "Feel free to share some story here."

"Well, I thought I was being noble in tossing an old flame a lifeline while she was in a tough place."

He shakes his head. "The wounded animal will often bite the very hand that moves to heal it."

"Not only pierce the hand but also the heart."

He shakes his head. "Sometimes it is just better to surrender it all to the sea. Let it go." Kai point out across the turquoise waters. "Give it to Mother Maui."

The pineapple melts in my mouth and then these words come from my soul. "Kai, I am learning a lot these days… That attachment and love are often confused as one… yet are actually polarities… That true love never possesses… only propels… That every attachment is merely a contraction… While true love always expands.

"To me love feels complete…and like the sun it shines of its own accord… Love is ultimate freedom…"

He raises his hand slowly towards the heavens. "To me it is the wind beneath an eagle's wings... The first breath of babies... and the last sigh of the dying..."

A colorful monarch butterfly wanders past us, lands for a moment, then takes wing again and disappears amongst the hibiscus.

He points toward the tiny creature. "Love is like that butterfly. If you chase her, she will elude you... for she cannot be held... If you catch her, she will be wounded and rendered flightless... If you hold her too tightly, she will be crushed and eventually die..."

I let the depth of his words sink into me and feel a tear slowly make its way down my cheek. "So seek not the illusion of ownership..."

He places his warm hand on my heart and whispers. "Yes brother man, seek not the illusion of ownership..."

"Mahalo, my friend... for all of it."

He considers me. "You are a different man from the one I found wandering by the airport curb that bright December day. Mother Maui has changed you-I believe for the better."

"Definitely for the better."

"A hui hou kakou... or until we meet again."

"Amen." I give him a hug. "And here I thought I was simply stopping for some pineapple."

He flashes a wide smile. "Life is full of beautiful surprises."

I wave goodbye and get back on my scooter. With a strong wind in my face, I ride out as far as the road will take me.

There I sit in meditation and listen to the island speak to my soul.

Stand in the bright light of your Infinite Being...

Let the Great Essential Sun

Shine upon your face...

Extend an open hand... an invitation...

As a safe place for True Love to land and rest from the demons of the world...

Give thanks for the time she shares with you...

Whether for a moment, or an all-too-brief lifetime...

For what is time between soul mates?

But a shadow passing momentarily in front of the Infinite Radiance of Being...

Give thanks for her Grace...

For in Her Presence the hole in all men vanishes and is filled...

Overflowing now in warmth and bliss...

Where once only tears existed...

Honor the gift and grieve its earthly passing...

But only briefly...

For soon new life will grow abundantly from the ashes of your sorrows...

Love, like the butterfly, is transformative... and everlasting...

Let Love go and let Love be...

For she will always come again.

The Homestretch

I return to the house to find her four large suitcases spread out across the room. In seven short days The Mirage has gone from a welcome guest to Maui pariah.

What is there to say?

She is in the process of packing and seems to be making the best of it. I realize that over the past couple of years, she had been asked to leave by several people, several times.

The sad life of a refugee...

Another part of me marvels at her ability to survive.

She appears relaxed despite not having a cent in the bank, debt collectors stalking her, and a dependence on substance. I know billionaires who are more anxious.

Ironically this constant state of self-created chaos is where she is most comfortable. How else to explain the ongoing need to recreate it?

In between sifting through her life's possessions, she picks up the phone and responds to the never-ending stream of Adderall-inspired texts.

I sit in the corner on a wicker chair like Michael Corleone did in *The Godfather*. Part of me wants to shake her out of all this madness, the same way I tried to years ago, but I know now that nothing could break through.

Somewhere in the back of my head, the jukebox of my mind is spinning the Simon and Garfunkel classic song, *The Sound of Silence.*

She fills me in on the latest plan. In an hour or so, some people she has never met, with a loose connection to Adderall Man, are coming to get her.

After a little more rearranging, she lets out a big sigh, sits down on the bed, and turns towards me. I look into those beautiful eyes that hold so much sadness and see a million uncried tears.

The pain I saw that first night in Del Mar has only deepened.

I remember for years trying desperately to ease her suffering, but through my own ignorance and inadequacy, only made things worse. This, among all things, pains me the most. Unfortunately her live-grenade approach to life triggers every one of my safety mechanisms.

Yet somehow through it all and even now, I still love her.

This is a great mystery to me. It defies everything rational and makes no logical sense. I don't even like her anymore. But I love her. Crazy. The mystery of love-good luck figuring that one out!

She looks up at me. "When you go, what do you plan to do with your bicycle?" She is being evicted but it doesn't alter her unquenchable sense of entitlement.

"I was planning to sell it. Why?"

"Maybe Adderall Man can buy it from you. How much did you want?"

At this point it was obvious to me that there is a wire loose somewhere in the hard drive. But I decide to go with it. "Sure. $150."

"Great. He could use a way to get around. Can he pay you later?"

I crack up. "You're kidding me."

"He will pay. I give you my word."

Now that is REALLY funny.

"Cash, and only cash my friend. Besides, I'm not sure a beach cruiser is the best means of transportation when dealing illegal medications. You never know when you might need to make a quick getaway."

She continues packing oblivious to my barbs. "Oh, can you go out to the garage and find me a box?"

My inner alarm knows she is trying to get me out of the room to make a grab, but for what? I had already hidden my computer, power chords, checkbooks, wallet, and even the sunscreen. *Playing along...* "Sure, what size?"

Without missing a beat, "Oh, about this big." She holds her hands out about a foot apart. "Nothing too big."

I act like I am garage bound, count to five, and peak back around the corner to see her scurry into the bathroom and quickly return with a handful of towels. She then stuffs the stolen booty into one of the bags and closes the top down.   This is tragic.

I return and open the suitcase. "Hey, what's this? You stole some towels?"

Then without a hint of any remorse, "There are so many of them here. I'm sure the house will go on with a few less."

I decide to let her keep the towels, but quickly look around my room again to see if anything else has been slipped into one of the four gigantic bags.

Glancing at the 'borrowed' computer on the bed I inquire, "Is this still on Craigslist?"

"No, I took it down. Which reminds me, I need to send it to her after I get a job and a place to live. She called and asked me about it. I feel terrible having taken it."

You got busted so you have to give it back.

I try to look on with my empathetic face. "Yes, I am sure you do. It must be extremely upsetting ~~to get caught and have~~ to return it.

She picks it up and places it in the stolen case. In the meantime, her phone is going non-stop: ringing, texts, and other funky sounds. Adderall Man is trying to hook her up with a ride coming from the far side of the island. "Can I call him?"

"Of course." I glance around the room to make sure there isn't anything in jeopardy of being lifted and then exit.

When I come back a few minutes later, they are talking on FaceTime but she has changed into her super sexy hot bikini black lingerie. She looks amazing and is obviously showing Adderall Man what delights await him for his devotion and ~~foolishness~~ chivalry.

If she had broken this little ensemble out earlier in the week, I may have been a few thousand lighter in my own savings account. Unfortunately, my presence ruins their little party but not before I hear him shout from the tiny phone, "Will you cyber fuck me again later?"

Again? That means at some point during this... oh whatever...

I'm sure the poor chap is completely hooked, just like I once was. She confirms this in a rare moment of candor when they hang up. "Poor Adderall Man, I'm pretty sure I could do anything, even break up with him and be with you, and he would still take me back."

The Mirage decides to keep her outfit intact and make another pitch. "This just feels wrong. I mean, what are we doing here? We can't blow this again."

God, she is so sexy and I know what she's after. Try not to cave. Remember the Alamo, or something. But what a body!

I nod earnestly but consciously choose to sit in the desk chair rather than on the bed next to her, where I would have been much easier prey. Funny how our primal survival instincts are always there to serve us.

Suddenly, the hallowed eyes of The Ghost of the Cautionary Tale flash before me, as parts of his story drift past me like the charred pieces of wreckage from some vessel that has been blown to bits: one night stand- 30 years of insanity- hundreds of thousands of dollars- life-ruining experience- aged me over a decade- one-night stand- pregnant- forever tied together- bi-polar tendencies...

"Pauly, is there any way you would help me? What about just giving me $800? That's what you pay for this room monthly. It'll set me up so I don't need him. I don't want him here with me..." The phone is still ringing and texting. "I better check it in case it's the people I'm supposed to stay with..."

I look at her. "Are you 100% sure he's not still on drugs or something?"

"He says he quit..."

Now back to business. She stands up, the much-too-small-by-design bra hopelessly inadequate to hold those magnificent breasts that are just a few inches from my mouth. "It's still not too late." She grabs something, and in a shot straight out of Playboy, bends over to put it away.

I feel like I am watching the Beatles record Abbey Road or Van Gogh paint. This is a master plying her craft.

The Ghost of the Cautionary Tale floats in again…One-night stand- 30 years of insanity- hundreds of thousands of dollars- life-ruining experience- radically aged me- one night stand- pregnant- forever tied together- bi-polar tendencies… borderline personality… criminal… run… never forget the pain…

Luckily the phone keeps going and is distracting enough to allow me not to be consumed or devoured.

Finally her potential life raft away from me is on the line, but there is a major glitch. She is welcome to stay with them, but they can no longer pick her up.

This opening invites a second round of persuasion.

Still clad in lingerie she begins brushing her hair out, "Can I stay here just one more night?" Now it was time for a little lotion on those tan legs, "They can't come get me and maybe this is the universe's way of giving us one more chance to figure this out."

Ah, the old Metaphysical New Age Grab Bag! I was waiting for that one to make at least some sort of cameo. I must admit part of me has a deep, perverse fascination with her and all of this. "Do you think so?"

She looks serious as she slowly rubs lotion on her inner thighs. "Yes, we need to get this straightened out."

The Ghost of the Cautionary Tale is in the fight of his life for my very soul…One-night stand- 30 years of insanity- hundreds of thousands of dollars- life-ruining experience- aged me a decade- one night stand- pregnant- forever tied together- bi-polar tendencies… run for your life, man!

Another text arrives on her phone and she reads it aloud. "Here is the address. If you can get here, you are more than welcome to stay. Aloha."

She sits back down on the end of the bed with those sad eyes trying to be brave, holding it all together yet again. What strength. She is so much stronger than I am. I admire her for this. She somehow always keeps going, ever hopeful that just around the corner there is someone who will change everything. If she can just keep going...

But now she rests just a couple feet from me. All that shared history in one tiny room filled with the four overstuffed suitcases.

Our eyes meet again, and I finally say something. "I'm really sorry."

"Me too." And with that, she put her head in her hands and breaks into deep sobs.

I move over and join her on the bed. I put my arms around her, holding her tightly.

The tears are contagious.

I cry for her, me, and for both of us. For what we did, and even more deeply for what we didn't do.

There are no words to say.

We crashed and burned this thing a long time ago and in the process threw away the great gift of deep love. We sit there like two ghosts mourning what was once alive in our corporal forms.

After a few moments the tears stop and we just hold each other.

She tries to dry her tears. "Why do I sabotage everything in my life?"

"Only you can answer that question."

"And now I am homeless, with nothing in the world."

Her phone dings again. Saved by the bell. "They want an answer. Can I stay here?"

I take a deep breath. "No. I'm sorry. Where is this place located?"

She looks down again. "Paia."

"That's not too far. Let me see if I can borrow the Cosmic Hoarder's car and drive you over." And with that, I bolt from her lingerie-clad form.

I find Cosmic in her usual state of complaining about someone taking wild advantage of her. Since she loves money, I take out a $20 bill and flash it in front of me. "Can I borrow your car for 90 minutes?"

Cosmic makes a funny face, glances back towards my room, and says, "Are you going to get rid of that sketchy girl?"

"Yes, as soon as possible."

"Good."

The Cautionary Tale himself looks up from the table and gives me an approving nod. He whispers the words, "I'm sorry, but it's for the best."

I give them both the thumbs up and Cosmic gives me the keys. I hand her the cash.

A few minutes later the tiny car is packed to the gills like The Grinch's sleigh as it approached the top of Mount Crumpet to dump it.

The Mirage is none too happy about any of this. "I still can't believe you are doing this to me."

"Do you feel you had any part in this unfolding?"

"No, not at all."

I shake my head. Where does one start any discussion when someone has such a mindset? I do not know what to say other than, "I'm really sorry you feel that way."

And I truly am, even though I could not drop this Spinning Vortex of Chaos off fast enough.

Part of me is terrified the car will break down on the way there; such is the power of the dark side.

Her phone never stops calling to her and she picks it up several times to chat with him, whisper, or say 'Give me a few minutes, I'm in the fucking car!'

Then suddenly, she has a new plan. "I don't want to stay with these people I don't know. I really don't like to impose on people."

Amazingly, she says that last line with a straight face.

"Okay then, where should I take you?"

"Let's take a look at that Hostel in Paia, maybe I will stay there for a night."

"Then you can have your cyber-sex date with Adderall Man."

"That's not why." She hisses. "I don't want to go somewhere where I'm not really wanted."

I decide not to pounce on that once-in-a-lifetime straight line. "To the hostel we go."

But not before driving around for over an hour lost, as she tries to find directions on her cell phone, while Adderall Man continues to call and text.

If I were watching this unfold on the big screen down at the multiplex, it would have been hysterical. But being trapped in the film as the distraught driver is not amusing.

As we circle in vain on the back roads of Paia, I begin to wonder if at some point I have passed through a portal and am now doomed to drive her around in this jalopy, while she texts and speaks in tongues for the rest of eternity.

After a few more hopeless laps, I realize this theory is actually fact and I am being punished for my every sin since the dawn of the universe.

My guess is at some point we will either run out of gas or bad karma. After stopping to ask a couple homeless stoners where this place might be, and then a dazed, barefoot Rasta carrying a drum, we finally find it.

For God's sake, can't we just bring Alan Funt out and end this thing?

The old structure looks scary and shaky, with a strong druggie vibe. So, in other words, it's perfect for her. She gets out and looks around, but refuses to stay there. "I can't stay here. I would be terrified. Can't I stay with you for one more night?"

"I'm sorry. My Cosmic Landlady said you had to be out. Call those friends again."

Her phone rings and, as we sit in the poorly-lit parking lot, she gives Adderall Man a blow-by-blow account of our last couple hours.

I am actually in hell. I probably entered hell about a week ago and have been unaware of my slow descent through Dante's levels of suffering although, we are obviously chartering new territory here. Since I am in Hades, I decide to start paying attention to the people who are walking past the car, assured that I may well witness some of history's most notorious figures: Hitler, Genghis Kahn, Dick Cheney...

After hanging up, she changes her mind again. "All right, take me to his friend's house."

About an hour later, we are looking for the place at the end of a very long road somewhere out by the airport.

Is it all a set up? Am I going to be murdered by drug thugs? At this point I decide that I would gladly welcome this outcome. At least it would finally put an end to this crazy day.

With the headlight beams on high, I drive happily toward my demise, comforted by the knowledge that all of my suffering will soon end. Then I have a scary thought: What if they lock me in a room with her overnight? Before I can decide what would be worse, we come upon a solitary dimly-lit home.

I quickly case the scene and decide the murderers are probably hiding behind the tall trees to the right, so I pull over as close to them as possible, if only to save all of us a little time. As we exit the car, a woman approaches with a welcoming presence. I'm still suspicious. Where are the killers? A young surfer appears who is as nice as the woman.

Then a beautiful white dog emerges who leans on me and licks my hand.

The moment right before my death... a white Angel disguised as a dog appears before me...

There are a few awkward moments of chatter, followed by vehicle unpacking, followed by the intrusive non-stop calling of someone in Honduras with way too much time on his hands.

They put the over-inflated suitcases into a rusty storage shed, while the lovely white dog leans against my right leg.

With the mist blowing across us as we are eerily illuminated by the lighting, it looks a lot like a poor man's ending to the film *Casablanca*, except this time the hero is anxious to see the girl go.

Still, my heart aches for her. After all, there is a human being standing over there, making stilted conversation with her New Host Organisms. A deeply broken and wounded person who I once loved uniquely and deeply.

Suddenly I find myself right back there in Del Mar, and she is walking through the front door, all smiles and ever so happy to meet me.

What a shame, what a sad and terrible shame, what a waste...

I notice her phone on the car seat still lighting up every few seconds.

A wave of compassion comes over me...

God Bless them both. Maybe they are actually good for each other in some strange way? Two refugees clinging together in pain in this lonely world... There is a human being on the other end of that phone somewhere in Central America who really loves this woman. Maybe he can do a better job than I did. I honestly hope so. Lord knows there is enough unhappiness in the world.

She comes back over to the car, grabs her beloved phone, checks the interior one more time in case she has forgotten anything, and then turns my way. "Well, I guess this is it. Can I call you tomorrow?"

"Please do. Let me know you are okay." I open my arms and she comes towards me. We hug tightly, but not for too long. It's hard enough already.

She lets go and walks back through the mist into her new life. Fortunately for me, the dog stays by me the whole time.

It occurs to me this is something akin to a hostage swap. I trade The Mirage and four of the largest suitcases I have ever seen for the return of my sanity and peace.

She turns at the entrance of the door, pauses in the mist, and waves goodbye. The door closes behind her and I am free to go.

am sure a new job from old friend. I don't worry. I know there is enough ration places in the world."

She came back over to the ... grab, her beloved phone, the ..., the intercom, no more time to ease she has to run for clothing and then ran on way. "Well, I have time to run. Can I tell you tomorrow?"

"Please, ... are you are make ... open my arms" and she comes for ... , me. We hug tight. "Adopted ... too long ... ahead, ... ahead already ..."

... and we walk back through the ... lobby ...
... ... field more ... to the ....

Because ... me this ... ... time of ... ...
.... him ... that ... them well ... of ... ...
.... on Park ... over ... day at the 1:00 ...

She knows the courage of the .... she ... this, more so today. Tea for the .... and never be ...

232

Sweet Shades

The next morning I sit at a small outdoor café across from the ocean as a warm sun cascades on my face. I hear a familiar voice. "How is life treating my fellow Red Sox fan?"

I open my eyes from my daydream. "Shades." I reach out and shake his hand. "So good to see you. Please join me."

He sits down.

I offer, "Would you let me buy you some breakfast."

"But I think it is my turn."

"My friend, you are mistaken." The waitress comes over, refills my cup, and takes his order.

He tips his cap. "You are very generous, my brother."

"'Tis you who give'th to me, oh wise elder and great bearer of wisdom."

Shades looks around the café and then leans in. "So what happened to the pretty girl?"

I grimace and shake my head. "She chose the other guy."

"The Adderall addict?"

"Yes."

He looks off across the park, past the palm trees, to the ocean. "Addicts choose addictions, not people. They are two of a kind. You are clean and clear. That's not where she is or what she wants. Her addiction made the choice, not her heart. I've seen it many times. It's not personal, but man, it can sure sting like it is. You must be hurting."

"I am. It was quite a week."

"One week; is that all it was?"

"Yes. Seven crazy days on Maui."

He takes a sip of his black coffee, lifts the cup towards me and says, "Sounds like a good title for a book. Well, you packed a lot in. She took you to school and back."

The warm ocean breeze blows softly over me. "I do feel like I got my PhD in crazy."

"You did and I still think you got off light. Not to pry, but did you sleep with her?"

"No, but man there were moments I really wanted to. Shows you how fucked up I am."

"Nonsense. Of course you did. You are a mammal just like those 60 ton whales roaming around out there." He points towards the sea. "There will always be the primal pull. Be thankful there is no child between you and for the valuable lessons garnered."

"Amen."

He ponders the moment. "I've been thinking about her. Here's my take: addiction is born out of a lack of love, compassion, and safety. It sounds like your girl has been on the run since the day she was born. Take it from someone who lives beneath the stars, it's tough to find any peace if you don't feel safe. The best we can do for her is a whole lot of empathy. You gave her a shot at a better life, so don't be too hard on yourself. I doubt you will repeat this experience with someone else."

The waitress brings him his scrambled eggs. "Oh, before I dig into this delicacy, there is something I found and cut out for you." He ferrets around in his tattered bag and pulls out a page from a magazine. "Here you go."

I put my hand on my heart. "You saw this and thought of me? How kind."

"Come on, we are friends. Please read the part I highlighted aloud for both of us.

"It is a quote from José Micard Teixeira.

> *'I no longer have patience for certain things, not because I've become arrogant, but simply because I reached a point in my life where I do not want to waste more time with what displeases me or hurts me. I have no patience for cynicism, excessive criticism and demands of any nature.*

I lost the will to please those who do not like me, to love those who do not love me and to smile at those who do not want to smile at me. I no longer spend a single minute on those who lie or want to manipulate. I decided not to coexist anymore with pretense, hypocrisy, dishonesty and cheap praise. I do not tolerate selective erudition nor academic arrogance. I do not adjust either to popular gossiping. I hate conflict and comparisons.

I believe in a world of opposites and that's why I avoid people with rigid and inflexible personalities. In friendship I dislike the lack of loyalty and betrayal. I do not get along with those who do not know how to give a compliment or a word of encouragement. Exaggerations bore me and I have difficulty accepting those who do not like animals. And on top of everything I have no patience for anyone who does not deserve my patience.'

"Shades, that is amazing and obviously quite timely."

"Please keep it. So how much longer are you hanging around on this old lava rock?"

"About a week, then it's off to Los Angeles."

He takes a long, slow sip of his black coffee. "You certainly will be missed around these parts. Do you think you might return?"

"Maybe. I'll migrate here once a year like the whales."

We finish and the busboy clears away our plates while Shades gets another refill on his java roast. "Before we part I must keep with our tradition and share a little something from my journal here."

"Of course." I lean back and soak in the moment.

He opens it to a marked page. "Here we go...

'The cool night air cascades off the Atlantic Ocean and catches up to me on a remote stretch of unspoiled beach. I'm seated in front of a roaring bonfire, staring into the shifting and lifting embers. This primal fire beneath the untamed stars feels healing for my soul.

And why is an open fire such a rare occurrence in our lives? In our effort to conquer nature, did we kill off an essential part of us? When did this great disconnect occur?

Long domesticated, most of us now sit trapped in towers with windows that never open in an anonymous array of dehumanizing cubicles. A somnolent hive of drones, we diligently burn away our precious lives on work with no connection to our souls.

Sitting a few feet from the blaze, I feel a force rise within me. Something ancient is stirring and ascending to the surface. Are these Spirits from the past, ready to emerge from within my modern persona?

These powerful forces that stir within me cravenly long for a kind of freedom that cannot be found in the castrated world of concrete.

I must get up and move.

I take a marathon walk along the ocean's edge and eventually collapse into the dunes. I gaze in awe at the diamond sky, the Milky Way's infinite suns.

A beam of light travels 186,000 miles a second. The nearest star other than the sun, Alpha Centauri, is about four light years away.

I ponder the unimaginable astronomical expanse in front of me and feel hopelessly insignificant. My casual cares and concerns vanish instantly when placed in proximity to such unlimited space.

Carl Sagan once said,

"For small creatures such as we the vastness is bearable only through love."

He closes with, "Amen…"

"Shades, those words are strikingly familiar…"

A small grin spreads across his face. "I would hope…"

"So you read my book?"

"*Hitchhiking With Larry David.* I loved every word of it."

"Thank you, brother man. '*For small creatures such as we the vastness is bearable only through love.*' That one still resonates for me."

"Me too, my man. You were generous to give it to me. It is being passed around the camp amongst our community and shared." He points back across the street, "You are quite famous over there…"

"Now that makes me feel even warmer than this radiant sunshine."

He reaches over and gently touches my arm. "Until the

next time…"

"I like that. It's much better than goodbye…"

He lowers his shades and looks me in the eye. "There are no goodbyes between friends, only pauses."

I walk across the street and take the sidewalk path along the shore. Eventually I find a shady spot in front of the Four Seasons to park myself and soak up the scene. A few minutes later a tall blond woman and six girls start posing for pictures on the green grass with the ocean in the background.

At some point the woman notices me and beckons me over with a request. "I hate to bother you, but do you mind taking a few pictures of us?"

"I'm not sure you can afford me," is my response.

She doesn't miss a beat. "What if I just want to do a short-term lease?"

"Depends on if you are local."

"Does LA count?"

"Actually it does. But it counts against you."

The woman is about fifty years old, six feet tall, with long straight blond hair, a model's build and a big smile. "What if I told you I was a native Hawaiian?"

"I would probably believe you."

She gives me a warm smile and holds out her camera. I take a whole lot of pictures of the gang as we all share the moment.

"And who are all these lovely young ladies?" I ask.

"I am the Queen, and these are my minions." The girls laugh and one of them says, "We are her daughters."

"All six of you? Are you pulling my leg?"

The Queen takes back her camera. "Nope. Three sets of twins."

I raise an eyebrow. "Talk about living large…"

Another one of the teenagers says, "Mom always does things in a big way. That's why we call her Queen D."

I let that sink in for a moment. "Queen D, didn't you release a couple of rap albums?"

She appears to enjoy the give and take. "You're funny…"

"Is there a King D or a prince of some kind?"

The Queen sticks out her tongue. "To be honest, the king is a crook and headed to jail. I've kissed a lot of toads, but so far not one of them has turned into a prince. It is just as well, since I have six daughters and three dogs. That's more than enough to keep me busy."

I shake my head. "You are living large."

She looks me over again. "So do you work here raking the leaves?"

I make a very serious face. "Don't let the low-key outfit fool you. I actually own the place."

She glances over my tattered clothes and beach sandals. "Are you sure you're not homeless?"

"Pretty sure. How about you? My guess would be Beverly Hills."

"Mom, he nailed it." A cute blond says.

Then Queen D asks, "Do you live here?"

I run my hand across the tropical horizon. "This has been my home for the past three months, but only for another week. Then it's off to Los Angeles."

Her girls begin to drift back up the stairs of the resort but she lingers behind for a moment. "May I ask what brings you there?"

"I have a book out that was bought and is now being released by a major publisher."

She lights up. "You're an author?"

"Yes. I wrote a memoir called, *Hitchhiking With Larry David*."

"Why are you going to Los Angeles?"

"My agent and publicist are based there, so I have to be around while the rest of the ride unfolds. They tell me that is where things are happening."

"Congratulations. I love to read. So how can I get a copy?"

For some reason and without a moment's hesitation, I reach into my backpack and hand her one of my test copies. "Here, you can have one of the preview printings."

"May I buy it from you?"

"This one's on the house, in case the pictures I took don't turn out well."

She flashes a big smile. "How generous. Are you sure?"

I give her a wink. "I've always had a soft spot for single moms."

She tucks it under her arm. "Thank you. How do I get in touch with you after I finish it?"

"My e-mail is in the back."

She spontaneously gives a light hug. "Well then, maybe I'll see you again."

"I hope so…"

Whale Wisdom

With my butt on a smooth piece of lava rock, and my feet in the sand, I nurse my morning espresso. I am down to my last 36 hours on the island.

The sun has yet to rise over the volcano and the water is like glass.

Stillness is everywhere.

A whale jumps in the distance. *Good morning!*

For some reason knowing they are out there brings me great comfort: so magnificent, so ancient, so mysterious.

I shut my eyes and feel something within me strongly call to get closer to them.

The next thing I know, I am paddling a single person kayak straight out off the South Kihei coast in search of giants.

A logical sounding voice within me speaks up: "Not to be an alarmist, but what the hell are we doing?"

The deepest part of me replies, *"We have to do this. Just relax, nothing can happen to us here."*

Logical Voice: "I think we are getting a little far from shore. What are we, about three miles out?"

"No worries, my friend…"

Logical Voice: "At least make sure your life vest is on tightly. Remember, these whales are close to 60 tons, and there are a lot of tiger sharks out here."

I paddle on and out. Soon the logical voice of fear accepts its place in the kayak and grows silent.

Glancing back at the now-distant shore, I am struck by the sheer beauty of the island.

The surface is unusually calm, but I know that fierce winds can kick up in moments with catastrophic consequences. I recall a story about a young couple being blown out to sea and never found.

I put my right hand in the water and offer a whale prayer. "Please come to me. I just wish to be near you. I am not entitled to your presence, yet it would be a great blessing for me…"

Be patient… comes the silent reply… be still…

Did I imagine that message?

Floating in this tiny piece of yellow fiberglass out on the lips of the mighty Pacific, I feel vulnerable and small.

Really, isn't it all so miniscule? All of my worries and cares, even those of the collective, are microscopic in relation to the scope of this magnificent planet… and this planet is just a tiny dot in a galaxy… and the Milky Way exists in something unimaginably vast…

Yet, I am somehow a tiny part of it all. In a sense, I come from the stars, at least the physical part of me. In fact, all of this beauty is stardust.

How crazy!

Though this fact exists 24/7, I marvel at how infrequently I consider the miraculous nature of stars colliding billions of years ago and in some mysterious way, creating my form. I look up at the radiant sun. 'That's a star!' A star! And all life here exists from…

Oh my God…

I am 'animated' stardust. The stars provide the clay, but the vessel is filled by something… mysterious… eternal…

Yes…

I didn't need to name it, or anything really. Naming it feels almost disrespectful, and radically limiting. I can just be 'aware' of it, and live in it, in the awe of…

POOOOOOOFFFFFFFF!!!!!

Like an explosion the sound startles me from my silent reverie.

Then another… POOOOOOOFFFFFFFF!!!!!

Thirty yards off the left of my bow, two majestic giants have emerged from the great depths of the sea to greet me. Have they heard my call and come?

The deep and vast sound of their breathing fills up the quiet morning.

The tide is pulling me directly towards them. Will I come upon their back? How would they react to such an intrusion?

Sixty yards directly in front of me a creature the size of locomotive shoots completely from the water, seems to momentarily defy gravity, and then crashes to the sea creating a sound not unlike a cannon firing.

Instinctively, I jump.

Watching them from the safety of the shoreline, they seem large, but here within earshot of their deep breaths and breeching, they are massive.

Their size and scope stretch my limited abilities of perspective.

For a moment I ponder the opportunities lost in relationship to these beings in the unconsciousness of our barbaric ignorance.

My mind flashes back to the nightmare of whaling ships, harpoons, immense suffering, of pain inflicted, of unimaginable genocide, and horrors. How could we? I know I could never harm something this sacred under any circumstances.

How tragic for them, and even more so for us.

As I drift within six feet of them, the two humpbacks sink silently beneath the surface.

A moment later, a much smaller version of the giants emerges directly to my right; it is a baby. I feel my heartstrings tug. As he swims towards the front of my craft, his mother appears on the far side of him and moves along in unison.

They submerge... then the original two escorts pop up to my right... the air again filled with the sound of oxygen being taken in and carbon dioxide being released.

Just like me, but on a much, much larger scale.

Should I be afraid? Does it even matter? So what if my puny little life were to end in this way. Fear cannot hold me or this precious moment hostage... I am truly free...

The twenty-foot whale bambino circles me, this time just a wee bit closer. Mom is somewhere under the water. I sense her presence and know she is close at hand. Another giant jumps nearby and crashes back to the water. BOOM! The other two adults are back within earshot.

Apparently the mothers swim all the way from Alaska, which is somewhere in the neighborhood of 3000 miles one way, to have their babies here in Maui. How do they find it? What guides them? How long has this been going on, a couple million years?

As another giant draws near me, I sense that these mysterious and ancient beings hold great secrets: stories of our planet, tales from unfathomable depths, lost civilizations and creatures long ago whose lives are unknown to our small scientific scope.

I become keenly aware that I am a guest here floating silently in hallowed waters.

The baby reappears and is now swimming backwards with his head out of the water around my kayak. His mouth wide open and he appears to be smiling.

We make eye contact and I feel goose bumps rise all over me.

What is he thinking? What do I look like to him? Does he wonder what my life above the water is like, as I contemplate his submerged world?

This moment is our sole point of intersection. After today, our lives will forever move in entirely different directions.

POOOOFFFF~!

The mother suddenly surfaces within thirty yards of me, hovers briefly in the water, and then begins to come straight towards my tiny vessel. If she keeps this course, I will be flicked aside as an afterthought.

I stop breathing. I feel a brief wave of terror. But soon the fear vanishes, and there is only reverence. I put my right hand on my heart and extended my left hand towards her. Every ounce of love in my Soul pours forth towards this Being.

I love you... I love you so much... I am in awe of you, I honor you, thank you... I love you...

As her mighty form gets much too close, she slightly submerges and then, in a timeless moment, passes directly underneath me.

The water on the surface above her takes on a surreal quality. She is just below the kayak, as a small stream of bubbles floats from her towards me. I put my hand into the water towards her giant yet gentle form and let the bubbles touch me. For just a second I see her beautiful eye, the portal to her Soul. A window to eternity...

The love from me intensifies and I realize there are tears streaming down my sunlit cheeks.

I lean further into the water and reach for her in vain.

My tears intensify and join the sea in a small offering of deep gratitude.

About forty yards away, she pops up again. But where is the baby? A moment later he comes up too...

Goodbye, my friends... again, thank you...

I sit out there and drift awhile. Then begin crying over the unimaginable beauty of it all. For life and for love, infinite love...

There is no hurry or desire to go back.

Yet, after a long stretch of drifting about beyond the confines of time, a linear construct begins to return along with the smaller concerns of my mammal self.

A few moments later I think about the Mirage.

The girl that I used to love madly is gone and so is the man known once as me.

I feel a deep wave of forgiveness.

For a moment I see her as a baby, so innocent and perfect. I wonder what had been done to this sweet creature to create such self-destructive madness? How could I offer anything but compassion for her and her journey?

And what is next for me?

I ponder this for a moment. To have any kind of agenda seems like a terrible violation of the infinite possibilities that eagerly offer themselves in every moment.

For a long time I just float there: free, weightless, and in awe of all that I can witness.

The sun has grown high in the sky and I know the midday winds will soon appear.

Do I have to return to land?

Yes, I have to bring these temporary things back to another reality: both the fiberglass kayak and my carbon-based life vessel.

Yet I know that something in me has been touched and changed in a way that will take a while to grasp.

Something died out here today, and something bigger was reborn within me.

I release the need to know and embrace the choice to love.

A Bittersweet Aloha

Sam I Am is scheduled to fly in from the Bay Area around 1:00 p.m. I will pick him up in his car, catch up over a healthy lunch, and then he will return me to the airport for my flight to California.

Everything works in sync as I arrive to find Sam waiting by the curb.

Thirty minutes later at Whole Foods he is finishing his lunch of fresh veggies and inquires. "I'm curious, did you get much writing done?"

"A ton. This new book is begging to be born. I owe the muse a debt of great gratitude."

He cocks his head. "The Broken Girl?"

"The gift that keeps on giving."

"I had a feeling." He pats me on the back. "You've used your time here well. Has it really been three months?"

"Funny Sam, it feels like days and yet also years. I feel ready for whatever is next."

"It's definitely your time to go." Shaman Sam stands up, "All right then. Let's get you to that plane."

I put my plate in the bin. "Let me hit the men's room first. You hang loose here."

The restrooms are behind a couple of doors near the meat department. I go through the portal and follow the red signs down a narrow stretch of valley separated by two mountain ranges of cardboard boxes.

I turn a corner and see a guy coming towards me followed by a woman. He looks familiar but from where? Then it hits me squarely.

Oh my God! There is no way this can be happening. I mean, what are the odds for this to occur? What the ???

He glances up, looks down, then suddenly jerks his head up and stops in his tracks a foot away with his mouth open.

Somehow I manage to find three words. "Yes, it's me."

Neither of us can say anything. Then he slowly extends his right hand towards me. "Well... hello."

I push his hand aside. "No handshakes here, my brother, just hugs." And with that I embrace him.

How wild!

The woman who was walking behind him realizes what is unfolding and gasps, "Oh...WHAT? NO WAY!"

I turn towards her. "How crazy for all of us. I guess we were supposed to finally meet."

She holds her hand to her mouth in shock, and then joins us in the tightest three-way hug in history.

Waves and waves of thoughts, feelings, beliefs, and ideas wash over and through me.

She cries, he leans into me, and I grip them both.

For a moment I feel like they belong to me, as if they are my children.

I'm not sure how long the three of us stand there: The Mirage, Adderall Man, and me, three small people on a path that happens to weave in out of each other's circle for a few moments of eternity.

Pure compassion flows through every fiber of my being.

In the dim of the fluorescent lights, Adderall Man looks a lot like Boo Radley in the heartbreaking film, *To Kill A Mockingbird*. He is small and holds a lot of pain in his dark and shaded eyes. Despite the tattoos and piercings, there is something fragile about him. Perhaps his pseudo tough guy persona is nothing more than a thin veneer of brave defense.

In an act of great generosity Adderall Man says, "Why don't I give you two an extra moment to say a proper farewell?" He then turns towards me and hugs me one more time. "Nice meeting you."

I feel terrible. Here I had all of these toxic assumptions and projections surrounding this person, and her too. Who am I to judge them, or anyone? I hug him. "Thank you..."

He squeezes me tightly and then lets go. Turning to her he says, "I'll meet you out by the car."

When he departs we just stand there for a minute and soak in our Divinely Ordained Encounter. We hug a couple of times and exchanging 'I love you's.'

I kiss her softly on the cheek, tasting a salty tear. "What a crazy love story," I whisper. "Are you doing all right?"

"Pauly, it's been hard. I won't lie. I think about you, I miss you, and I understand now what you were trying to express to me. I wish we had more time to work through it. We have wasted so much time. That is what always makes me saddest: what we lost and what could have been."

"Yes, my dear, so much has been lost..."

She leans into me. "Ironically, I am living about 100 yards away from your place, right up on the hill. The house is seedy with no electricity, but we are on the lookout for better things. Perhaps one morning we could meet for a walk?"

I shake my head. "I'm leaving today, directly from here."

She looks startled, steps back, and reaches for me. "Oh my God, that breaks my heart."

"I guess our souls wanted to say goodbye and share one last hug."

"You can't leave... I mean, I need..." She is crying on my shoulder. "Please promise me you will stay in my life?"

"Miracle, try to remember that we will always be together in some way, even if we never see each other in these forms again. A portion of us, our Essence really, is always connected."

I reach into my pocket, "Here..."

She's surprised. "$200 dollars? For what?"

"A simple gift to love."

"For me?"

"Yes, and him." I put my hands around her tiny hand with the money in it. I pause for a moment to consider things. "Be good to him, be generous, and be kind. He is fragile. The world has enough pain in it to last for a million years. If you can, try not to add any more to it."

"I love you, Pauly. I already miss you." She takes a few steps, stops, and then comes back to me. "Wait a second..." She reaches into her purse, takes out a very small velvet pouch and opens it. "Please, take this..."

It is a small key with emeralds and other jewels on it.

She puts it in my hand. "This is the key to my heart."

"Are you sure?"

"I brought it to Maui with the intent to give it to you. It never felt right until this moment."

I examine it, so small and frail, almost like her really. "It has a stone missing."

"I know; it fell out…"

"How perfect… it's broken, just like us."

She reaches up and lingers a kiss on my cheek. With one long hug we part. I watch her pass through the twin doors and once again out of my life.

Crazy…

Suddenly The Inner Hole pops up, "I gotta say, kid, I can't believe *that* just happened."

"What, us running into them here amongst all these boxes, right before I take off?"

"No, silly, you giving her $200 for no reason."

I laugh out loud. "That's a good one. You know you're not really half bad…"

"Now don't start bringing all that love and compassion my way. You'll destroy me, you know…"

"I'm sorry. Why does all this remind me of the end of *Casablanca?*"

"Our favorite movie…"

"Yes, remember the last scene where Rick walks away with Inspector Renault…"

The Hole says, "Except this time instead of fog, the star-crossed lovers are surrounded by cardboard…"

Who knew the Hole could be so funny?

The Hole adds, "You let her go. That's true love…"

I pause to ponder this. "Perhaps another book?"

"Yes, in lieu of real work…"

"There you are!"

"Hey, I can't grow soft on you. Who's going to keep you on your toes and kick your sorry ass? You're arrogant enough…"

I shake my head and smile, "There's no arguing with you…"

"Well, that's no fun… you know I was thinking, why the hell did you ever…"

When I return, Sam I Am asks, "Where in heaven's name were you? I got a little worried."

I glance out the window. There, across the parking lot, getting into an old rusted car, were the two of them. The refugees. Yet now they are smiling and shaking their heads.

Sam interrupts my daydream. "Hello… earth to Paul…"

I put my arm around his shoulder and point towards the jalopy as it begins to drive off. "It's a very long story."

He pauses for a moment, looks towards the car, gets a sly look on his face, and then smiles. "I hope you're going to write it all down."

"That appears to be the plan."

A few hours later, somewhere over the Pacific Ocean between Maui and California, I open my eyes and see a very attractive blond flight attendant standing over me smiling. "Well, it looks like someone has finally woken up."

Postscript

*Tonight I can write the saddest lines
That I loved her, and sometimes she loved me too
On nights like this one, I held her in my arms.
I kissed her again and again under the endless sky
She loved me, and sometimes I loved her too*

How could one have not loved her great, still eyes?

*To think that I do not have her
To feel I have lost her
To hear the immense night
Still more immense without her
And the verse falls to the soul like dew to the pasture*

What does it matter that my love could not keep her?

*The night is shattered, and she is not with me
This is all. In the distance someone is singing*

*My soul is not satisfied that it has lost her
My sight searches for her as though to go to her
My heart looks for her, and she is not with me*

Pablo Neruda

~~~

When my plane lands I make a spontaneous decision to delay Los Angeles and head south on the 405 Freeway.

I drive through the night and arrive in Del Mar well after midnight. After checking into a small hotel and a long, hot shower, I venture out under a panoramic sky for a long walkabout along the beach.

The moon is full and the tide exceptionally low.

For timeless miles I journey along the water's edge.

The wind is aggressive and it howls through me.

Memories of my time here with her wash over me like the cold surf on my feet: the meandering walks taken on these very sands, the unscripted laughter and the tears of growth. There were plans made and dreams forsaken, insights gathered and opportunities lost.

All of it carried and scattered by the warm, moist air.

Somewhere out across the vast ocean covered in moonbeams, she lies sleeping in the arms of another man, perhaps dreaming of better days and a life of less sorrow.

At some point the sky begins to turn shades of shifting pink as the sun rises out of the scope of my view.

As the last of the long night vanishes, I come upon a large rock where she and I sat on our first full day of connection.

How many years have passed from that precious sunset?

All of it now a blur within me… a mystical dance of shadows and light flickering faintly in the corners of my mind…

I suddenly feel compelled to travel back in time and warn those two sweet people on the boulder of the vast pitfalls and challenges that lie ahead of them, to always put each other above all else, and though their love is powerful, she is as fragile as a newborn's breath.

My current insights, crudely born from the crucible of pain and long nights like this one, spent wandering across the emotional landscape.

I take a deep breath and summon enough courage to sit upon the majestic rock.

As the outermost tip of the sun appears above the mountains, I move back in time and we are once again holding hands while watching the waves touch the sand.

Was that the evening we decided she should come back with me to Nashville?

Or the time she sobbed soulfully on my tattered linen shirt over the pain she carried like a cross to Calvary?

Oh Lord, my precious girl…

I dry my eyes and reach into my right pocket. I hold tightly the tiny key with the missing stone.

"Thank you, dear one, for the glory of it all. The smiles and pain… thank you."

I kneel down and dig a small grave in the moist sand. My hands shake as I carve out a sacred resting place for what once mattered most.

I place the tiny key into the womb of the earth.

My tears trickle into the sand as I give it all back.

My own words wash over me...

Give thanks for the time she shared with you...

Whether for a moment, or an all-too-brief lifetime...

For what is time between soulmates?

But a shadow passing momentarily in front of the Infinite Radiance of Being...

The tide rushes in over my freshly buried treasure.

I look up the hill and see the faint outline of the house where we met and later occupied.

In no small irony, the place is almost completely dismantled, as if only a temporary set piece in an elaborate movie that has long ceased filming.

Another wave comes in...

The time and tide are advancing, and so must I.

I take one more deep breath, then gently leave the past forever.

As three large pelicans glide silently above me, I take my first step toward higher ground.

Acknowledgements

Thank you...

To all the amazing people who have read my books, *Hitchhiking With Larry David & Martha's Vineyard Miracles*, and let me know how much my words meant to you - through countless notes, long hugs, chance encounters, heartfelt stories and magical moments shared in presence.

Your love and support empowered me to write the book you are holding in your hands.

I hope you will stay in touch.

To my oldest friends who also happen to be my amazing parents, I love you deeply.

Your life of sacrifice and service enabled me to embody a life of opportunity & infinite possibilities. You taught me that with enough hard work, any dream was within my grasp.

Lastly, your sixty-nine year love affair is a monument to caring and commitment. I feel blessed to not only be a witness to your story, but a living example of it.

Saint Katherine of Lott... my spiritual sister in laughter, learning, love and mischief... Thank you for stepping up and filling the world with healing light... Everything you touch improves and glows...

To a large group of Angels cleverly disguised as my beautiful friends. It has been such a privilege to be a part of your lives.

In no particular order...

To the Great Simmons and his lovely family. David, I appreciate your support and guidance, and all of your creative suggestions.

Annie Pie, you are such a sweet soul and you always give 1000% so graciously.

James Weinberg for all the support and fellowship.

Karen B. you found the dream my friend.

Brother Malcolm for the endless hours we share and grow together. Ma Bevins...! Montanez Wade Norm the Giver and his wonderful partner Jane... Kevin & Tahra, Merilynn & Romantic Mike.

Vineyard Family: Ann & Mark Ide, Rita and Frank on Circuit, Terrell & Kim, Priscilla and Ned, Water Street Wendy also known as Cindy, Tony on 19th Street, Rabbi Jim, Wingman Kevin and the beautiful Ali & Tim, Pat and April, Vasska and Tarni, Suzanne, & Colin- thanks for taking care of my jeep!

To the wonderful people at the Edgartown Bookstore, who have created a magical oasis for all of us to bask. Way to go Joyce & Jeffrey!

Alan Brewer, my long time friend who gave me a home in the city of angels as well as a robust friendship. I am so happy you found Angel Susan!

David Sanford-my brother from another mother...

Jill McClure and her clan- Luci & Sam, Gracie,

Neil Warren, Robert Matsuda...

Nashville: Lucas P. Gravel, Saint Dennis Martin, Dan Maddox, Mike Bodayle, RC Morton...

My Beloved Bonnie Johnson... for the endless hours of love, support, and healing!

Angel Barb & Izzy in Maui... you embody the Aloha... You too Autumn Shields!

JP Sears, you are so gifted!

Gracie and The Monkeys

Matthew Wayne Selznick, who makes everything I do look and sound better. Thank you for creating such a lovely cover. Bravo!

Peter Dergee! My dear friend, brother and producer extraordinaire, thank you.

To all the amazing people who continue to bare their souls on The Pauly Cast- I am honored to share a little space with you on this magical ride.

Please stay in touch!

Send me your Miracle stories

Email:

mvyhitchhiker@gmail.com

Please visit my site:

www.paulsamueldolman.com

Facebook:

http://www.facebook.com/home.php?#!/profile.php?id=731140460

Twitter:

psdhitchhiker@twitter.com

www.ingramcontent.com/pod-product-compliance
Lightning Source LLC
Chambersburg PA
CBHW071000160426
43193CB00012B/1855